Coastal Tourism, Sustainability, and Climate Change in the Caribbean, Volume I

Coastal Tourism, Sustainability, and Climate Change in the Caribbean, Volume I

Beaches and Hotels

Edited by
Martha Honey, PhD
with Samantha Hogenson
Center for Responsible Travel (CREST)

BUSINESS EXPERT PRESS

CREST
Center for Responsible Travel

Coastal Tourism, Sustainability, and Climate Change in the Caribbean,
Volume I: Beaches and Hotels
Copyright © Business Expert Press, LLC, 2017.
Center for Responsible Travel (CREST), 2017.

First published in 2017 by
Business Expert Press, LLC
222 East 46th Street, New York, NY 10017
www.businessexpertpress.com

Center for Responsible Travel (CREST)
1225 Eye Street, NW, Suite 600
Washington, DC 20005

ISBN-13: 978-1-63157-473-3 (paperback)
ISBN-13: 978-1-63157-474-0 (e-book)

Business Expert Press Tourism and Hospitality Management Collection

Collection ISSN: 2375-9623 (print)
Collection ISSN: 2375-9631 (electronic)

Cover and interior design by S4Carlisle Publishing Services
Private Ltd., Chennai, India

First edition: 2017

10 9 8 7 6 5 4 3 2 1

Printed in the United States of America.

Dedication

*For the innovative leaders in sustainable tourism
who have seen the realities of climate change and are
proactively working to find solutions.*

Abstract

The Caribbean is the most tourism-dependent region in the world, with an average of 50 million visitors a year. Most of its tourism infrastructure, including its 2,600 hotels as well as nearly three-quarters of its people, are concentrated along its coastlines. While the Caribbean island nations contribute less than 1 percent of carbon emissions to global climate change, they are among the most vulnerable to its impacts, including increasingly fierce and frequent hurricanes, sea level rise, hotter temperatures, and loss of coral and mangroves. Yet many vacationers, home owners, governments, and tourism developers and operators fail to fully grasp the realities of climate change.

Two truths run through the essays and case studies in this edited volume: one, many of these environmental problems predate but are exacerbated by climate change, and two, many of the techniques for mitigating and adapting to climate change are part of the tool kit of sustainable tourism that has been honed over recent decades. Therefore, companies and coastal destinations adhering to the socially and environmentally sustainable practices such as beach setbacks, soft engineering, renewable energy, water recycling and reduction, and "green" architecture are likely to be more resilient in coping with climate change. Tourism master planning and building today requires *a new normal* that incorporates present risks and climate change protections using smart planning, sustainable design, and responsible construction.

This book focused on beaches and hotels and its three companion volumes are designed for use in university courses (both graduate and undergraduate), as well as by tourism businesses, practitioners, and associations; governments; international finance and development agencies, and concerned travelers.

Keywords

Adaptation, Caribbean, certification, climate change, coastal tourism, hotels, mitigation, resilience, resorts, responsible tourism, sea level rise, sustainable development, sustainable tourism

Contents

Foreword and Acknowledgments

The idea for these volumes on coastal tourism and its companion volumes on marine tourism grew out of the 2015 "Innovators Think Tank: Climate Change and Coastal & Marine Tourism" held in Punta Cana, Dominican Republic, July 22–24, 2015. Organized and hosted by the Center for Responsible Travel (CREST) and the Puntacana Ecological Foundation and its Director Jake Kheel, the Think Tank brought together some 35 sustainable tourism practitioners and climate change experts to take stock of how coastal and marine tourism in the Caribbean is currently dealing with climate change and its impacts and to identify priorities that still need to be addressed. Our discussions, ably facilitated by Roger-Mark De Souza of the Woodrow Wilson Center, were organized around a single critical theme: *How coastal and marine tourism must be planned, built, and operated in this era of climate change.*

One outcome of the Think Tank was the unanimous decision to put together a publication on the same theme as a tool for public education. As testimony to the importance and urgency of this topic, our publication gradually expanded into four volumes focused on Caribbean coastal and marine tourism. We are grateful that many of the Think Tank participants agreed to contribute by writing essays and case studies for these four volumes. Additional authors were identified during the year that we have worked on these volumes. All generously contributed their expertise to this common project.

Early in the process, as well, Kreg Ettenger, associate professor of anthropology at the University of Maine, graciously agreed to come on board as editor of the marine volumes and collaborator for all four volumes. His contributions have been enormous and have added greatly to the quality of both books.

Indispensable as well to this project has been Samantha Hogenson, CREST's managing director, who not only contributed to the concept and content, but also, with her usual efficiency, oversaw the final copyediting and assembling of all the components of the manuscript. She also oversaw the CREST researchers who have worked diligently on numerous essential but often tedious details. Patricia Núñez Garcia, who was part of the CREST team at the Think Tank, transcribed a number of presentations that have been reshaped into contributions for the manuscript. Ashley Newson and Helena Servé organized all the photos and graphics, including successfully securing permissions for each of them. Helena also stepped in to assist with numerous research tasks as well as some of the copyediting. The bulk of the copyediting for this volume was done remotely by Ryan Davila, a PhD candidate at Arizona State University.

Finally, four other CREST researchers, Gabriela Aguerrevere Yanez, Angela Borrero, Noora Laukkanen and Emily Simmons contributed to tracking down information, researching topics, and identifying potential authors. We are grateful to this entire team!

We would like to thank Scott Isenberg and Business Expert Press for taking an early interest in our proposal and agreeing to publish these volumes. We were fortunate to make contact just as BEP was launching its Tourism and Hospitality Management Collection, and to find that, like CREST, BEP focuses on reaching academic and business audiences. We are also grateful to the collection editor, Betsy Stringam of New Mexico State University, for her helpful comments and enthusiastic reception of our manuscripts and Charlene Kronstedt, BEP's Director of Production, for her careful guidance in completing the final manuscript.

We thank these contributors and collaborators one and all, and hope that they will be as pleased with the final product as are we at CREST.

—Martha Honey
Editor and CREST Executive Director

Key Definitions

Adaptation: The adjustment in natural or human systems in response to actual or expected climatic stimuli or their effects, which moderates harm or exploits beneficial opportunities.[1]

Caribbean: According to the United Nations, the Caribbean region consists of: Anguilla, Antigua and Barbuda, Aruba, The Bahamas, Barbados, Bonaire, Sint Eustatius and Saba, British Virgin Islands, Cayman Islands, Cuba, Curaçao, Dominica, Dominican Republic, Grenada, Guadeloupe, Haiti, Jamaica, Martinique, Montserrat, Puerto Rico, Saint-Barthélemy, Saint Kitts and Nevis, Saint Lucia, Saint/St. Martin (French: Saint-Martin and Dutch: Sint Maarten)[i] Trinidad and Tobago, Turks and Caicos Islands, and United States Virgin Islands.[2]

CARICOM: CARICOM Member States are Antigua and Barbuda, The Bahamas, Barbados, Belize, Dominica, Grenada, Guyana, Haiti, Jamaica, Montserrat, Saint Lucia, St. Kitts and Nevis, St. Vincent and the Grenadines, Suriname and Trinidad and Tobago. Associate Member States are Anguilla, Bermuda, the British Virgin Islands, the Cayman Islands and the Turks and Caicos Islands.[3]

Certification: A voluntary procedure that assesses, monitors, and gives written assurance that a business, product, process, location, or management system conforms to specific requirements. It awards a marketable logo or seal to those that meet or exceed baseline standards, i.e., those that at a minimum comply with national and regional regulations and, typically, fulfill other declared or negotiated standards prescribed by the program.[4]

Climate Change: A change in global or regional climate patterns, in particular a change apparent from the mid to late 20th century onwards and attributed largely to the increased levels of atmospheric carbon dioxide produced by the use of fossil fuels.[5]

---

[i]The island is divided 60 /40 between France (Saint Martin) and The Netherlands (Sint Maaren). It is the smallest inhabited island divided between two nations.

Global Warming: The recent and ongoing rise in global average temperature near Earth's surface. It is caused mostly by increasing concentrations of greenhouse gases in the atmosphere. Global warming is causing climate patterns to change. However, global warming itself represents only one aspect of climate change.[6]

Mitigation: The lessening or limitation of the adverse impacts of hazards and related disasters.[7]

Resilience: The ability to prepare and plan for, absorb, recover from, and more successfully adapt to adverse events.[8]

Responsible Tourism: Tourism that maximizes the benefits to local communities, minimizes negative social or environmental impacts, and helps local people conserve fragile cultures and habitats or species.[9]

Sea Level Rise: The so-called greenhouse effect or global warming may cause a Sea Level Rise, which will have a great impact on the long-term coastal morphology. The possible and gradual Sea Level Rise will cause a general shoreline retreat and an increased flooding risk and has to be handled according to the local conditions.[10]

Sustainable Development: Development that meets the needs of the present without compromising the ability of future generations to meet their own needs.[11]

Sustainable Tourism: Tourism that leads to the management of all resources in such a way that economic, social, and aesthetic needs can be fulfilled while maintaining cultural integrity, essential ecological processes, biological diversity, and life support systems.[12]

Notes

1. United Nations Office for Disaster Risk Reduction (UNISDR). (January 2009). https://www.unisdr.org/we/inform/terminology.
2. United Nations Statistics Division. Composition of macro geographical (continental) regions, geographical sub-regions, and selected economic and other groupings. http://unstats.un.org/unsd/methods/m49/m49regin.htm.
3. CARICOM. Member States and Associate Members. http://www.caricom.org/.

4. Martha Honey, ed. (2002). *Ecotourism and Certification: Setting Standards in Practice.* Washington, D.C.: Island Press. P. 380.

5. English Oxford Living Dictionary. "Definition of Climate Change." https://en.oxforddictionaries.com/definition/climate_change.

6. United States Environmental Protection Agency. "Climate Change: Basic Information." https://www.epa.gov/climatechange/climate-change -basic-information.

7. United Nations Office for Disaster Risk Reduction. (August 2007). https://www.unisdr.org/we/inform/terminology.

8. Urban Land Institute. (2015). *Returns on Resilience: The Business Case.* ULI Center for Sustainability. Washington, D.C.: Urban Land Institute. http://uli.org/wp-content/uploads/ULI-Documents/ Returns-on-Resilience-The-Business-Case.pdf.

9. City of Cape Town. (August 2002). Cape Town Declaration. https:// www.capetown.gov.za/en/tourism/Documents/Responsible%20 Tourism/Toruism_RT_2002_Cape_Town_Declaration.pdf.

10. Karsten Mangor. (2004). *Shoreline Management Guidelines.* UK: DHI Water and Environment. 294pp.

11. World Commission on Environment and Development. (1987). *Our Common Future.* Oxford: Oxford University Press. http://www.un -documents.net/our-common-future.pdf.

12. United Nations. Sustainable Development Knowledge Platform. https://sustainabledevelopment.un.org/topics/sustainabletourism.

List of Acronyms

AoE: Ambassadors of the Environment
CAST: Caribbean Association for Sustainable Tourism
CFC: chlorofluorocarbon
CFL: compact fluorescent lighting
CHENACT: Caribbean Hotel Energy Efficiency and Renewable Energy Action
CHP: combined heat and power
CHTA: Caribbean Hotel and Tourism Association
CPACC: Caribbean Planning for Adaptation to Climate Change
CREST: Center for Responsible Travel
CRI: Recycling and Incineration Center
CSR: corporate social responsibility
CTO: Caribbean Tourism Organization
DoE: Department of Energy/Environment
EbA: ecosystem-based adaptation
EIA: environmental impact assessment
EMS: Energy Management System
EPA: United States Environmental Protection Agency
FEMA: United States Federal Emergency Management Agency
GDP: gross domestic product
GHG: greenhouse gas
GIZ: German Agency for International Cooperation
GOPAR: Gross Operating Profit per Available Room
GPC: Grupo Puntacana
GSTC: Global Sustainable Tourism Council
HACCP: Hazard Analytics Critical Control Point
HEPA: High Efficiency Particulate Air
ICF: insulated concrete form
ISO: International Organization for Standardization
kWh: kilowatt-hour

LBC: Living Building Challenge

LED: light emitting diode

LEED: Leadership in Energy and Environmental Design

MESA: Managed Energy Services Agreements

MPA: marine protected area

NAMA: Nationally Appropriate Mitigation Actions

NGO: nongovernmental organization

PPA: power purchase agreement

PV: photovoltaic

REDD+: Reducing Emissions from Deforestation and Forest Degradation Plus

ROI: return on investment

SHW: solar hot water heating systems

SIDS: Small Island Developing States

SLR: sea level rise

ULI: Urban Land Institute

UNFCCC: United Nations Framework Convention on Climate Change

VRC: variant refrigerant flow

Map of the Caribbean

Map of the Caribbean Sea and its islands.

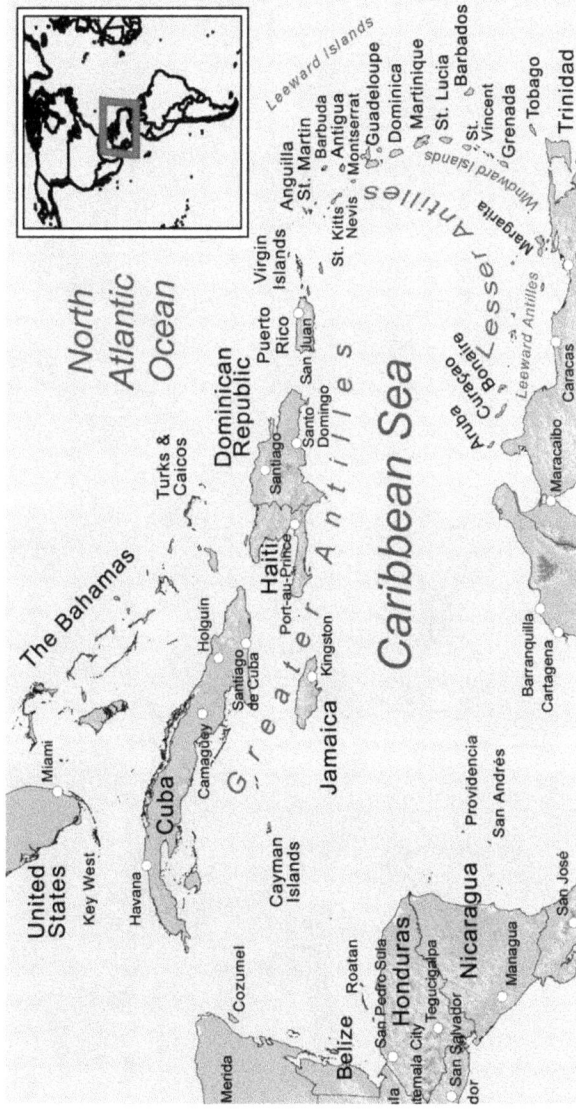

Source: Karl Musser, Creative Commons

CHAPTER 1

Introduction

Martha Honey

Coastal and marine tourism are the fastest growing sectors of the tourism industry. Beaches and coastlines are being rapidly bought up and built up by resort and vacation home developers, while the number, size, and ports-of-call of cruise ships are growing rapidly. Nowhere is this more apparent than in the Caribbean, the most tourism dependent region in the world. In 2015, for the first time, tourism in the Caribbean grew at a faster pace than any other region in the world. Typically, some 50 million overnight tourists and cruise passengers—most from the United States—vacation in the Caribbean each year. Yet large-scale, mass market, sun-and-sand tourism, the staple of much of the Caribbean, at times can cause a range of environmental and social problems.

In recent years, these Caribbean island nations have also become extremely vulnerable to climate change impacts, including sea level rise (SLR) and ocean warming, coral and mangrove destruction, increasingly fierce and erratic storms, and a host of other human-induced phenomena. As an industry, tourism both contributes to and is a victim of climate change. Given these realities, tourism cannot continue to pursue business as usual. Fortunately, as the essays and case studies in this and its companion volume demonstrate, there is today a growing number of sustainable tourism businesses that are providing social and environmental benefits to destinations and local communities.

This volume is the first of two on coastal tourism and is organized around a central theme: *How coastal tourism must be planned, built, and operated in this era of climate change.* While our focus is on the Caribbean, we have included for purposes of comparison a few case studies from other destinations that provide innovative and transferable applications for this region. In the two volumes on coastal tourism, the 30-plus authors who contributed overview essays and case studies include tourism practitioners, academics, scientists, and community and nonprofit leaders. In broad terms, we seek to look at four key questions surrounding tourism and climate change in the Caribbean:

- How do various sectors of coastal tourism contribute to climate change?
- How are the various sectors experiencing the impacts of climate change?
- What measures have tourism businesses (and governments) taken to date to address climate change?
- Given what climate scientists are predicting for the future, what are the main gaps between current best practices by tourism businesses and the changes required to effectively address climate change?

There are two truths that run through this and its companion volume on coastal tourism. The first is that many of the problems facing the Caribbean's natural environment predate but are exacerbated by climate change. Therefore, oftentimes the solutions to addressing problems such as coral die-offs or storm surges or fresh water shortages involve addressing multiple issues, not simply climate change. A second truth is that many of the techniques for mitigating and adapting to climate change are part of the tool kit of sustainable tourism that has been honed over recent decades by innovative companies and entrepreneurs, often backed by NGOs, researchers, scientists, governments, and international development agencies. Therefore, companies, communities, and coastal destinations that are already adhering to the principles and practices of sustainable development are likely to be more resilient in coping with climate change.

The following are brief synopses of each of this volume's chapters.

Chapter 2: Beach and Shoreline Protection

In the opening essay, Judi Clarke looks at the importance of beaches and shorelines as both the Caribbean's most important tourism asset and as the frontline in battle to confront climate change. For decades, beaches and shorelines have been facing pressures from natural forces and human impacts, including destructive and shortsighted tourism development. Now climate change is accelerating these pressures. Despite the realities of coastal vulnerability and loss, Clarke writes that "complacency continues to be the norm in much of the Caribbean." Beaches and shorelines are living, evolving ecosystems, and tourism's built structures often require different approaches to effectively cope with climate change impacts. Clarke describes four types of climate resilient interventions: setbacks and retreat, *build back better*, hard engineering, and soft engineering. While not all of these approaches embrace the concept of living shorelines, ultimately the most successful solutions incorporate a combination of these four approaches.

The case studies in this chapter highlight failures by vacation home owners, vacationers, and governments to fully grasp the realities of climate change. In the first case study, researchers found that less than 30 percent of home owners along North Carolina's Outer Banks believe that climate change will negatively impact property values over the next 25 years. The second case study finds that while available research is limited, sun-and-sand tourists appear to be intolerant of climate change realities: both beach erosion and hard engineering devices intended to preserve beaches and shorelines may cause tourists to stop visiting the destination. The longer term implications may be that tourists decide to abandon the Caribbean for other less impacted vacation spots. Finally, a case study of the Dominican Republic finds the government's strategy to expand the numbers of large all-inclusive resorts is straining coastal resources and not addressing the realities of climate change. In contrast, Counterpart International and local partners in the DR are piloting coastal and marine projects to expand nature-based community tourism and other sustainable economic activities. They have come to understand that active community participation is key for conservation, protection of local livelihoods, and successful adoption of climate change resilience strategies.

Chapter 3: Siting, Architecture, Design, and Construction

The overview essay by Denaye Hinds and Esteban Biondi argues that tourism master planning and building today requires a new normal that incorporates present risks and climate change projections using smart planning, sustainable design, and responsible construction. They argue that most coastal resorts in the Caribbean have not been properly designed to withstand present-day hurricane conditions, let alone the increased vulnerabilities due to climate change. The authors describe a range of new tools, policies, and certification programs designed to increase sustainability and resilience to climate change. These include legal setbacks from the high water mark, protection of open spaces, repurposing of existing sites and buildings, elevated construction, passive and flexible architectural designs, renewable energy, prefabricated buildings, and native and drought-resistant plants. They argue that tourism projects that incorporate sustainable and climate resilient innovations have the ability to *bounce forward* with recovery improvements after storms and flooding and also have increased value and longer life span.

The case study of the Ritz Carlton Grand Cayman outlines how, after the resort suffered severe hurricane damage, a team of experts developed a multipurpose recovery plan, including mangrove restoration, protective rock structures, and other measures that simultaneously provided resilience and improved amenities and activities, therefore making the project justifiable on both environmental and economic grounds. The case study of Sugar Ridge, a Green Globe certified boutique resort in Antigua, demonstrates how its mountain location provides a range of natural assets including wide vistas, ocean views, fresh air, lush vegetation, and range of non-beach activities. The third case study is of Via Verde, a sustainable and affordable mixed-used development built on a brownfield in the Bronx, New York, that fuses together natural and urban space. Unlikely as it sounds, this LEED-certified project encompasses architectural and construction principles and designs relevant to the Caribbean, including open space, green roofs, solar energy, water conserving plumbing, and other climate-resilient features.

Chapter 4: Coastal Hotel Chains and Independent Resorts

In her overview essay, Denaye Hinds reviews the forecasts of climate change impacts for Caribbean coastal tourism, including the loss of

150 resorts with a 2°C rise in global temperatures and damages totaling $22 billion a year by 2050. She then discusses a wide range of sustainable technologies and eco-certification programs that both independent boutique hotels and branded resort chains are using to reduce their own carbon footprint and to adapt their construction and operations to cope with climate change. Several Caribbean-wide initiatives, backed by governments, tourism associations, and international agencies, are also promoting transitions to more sustainable practices, especially for energy and water. Hinds concludes, "For every climate related challenge, there is, it seems, a solution." She says that going forward, "the mantra must be: Sustain, Elevate, Innovate."

The first case study discusses the disconnect in the time frame or ROI (return on investment) between guest facing and back of the house improvements and how Starwood properties are working to overcome this disconnect through a combination of environment goals, foundational initiatives, and innovative financing. The next case study describes how Ewald Biemans, owner of Bucuti & Tara Beach Resort in Aruba, has built a highly successful, award-winning *green* resort with an all-encompassing commitment to environmental and social sustainability and climate-resilient measures, including compliance to four international eco-certification programs. The third case study looks at Grupo Puntacana in the Dominican Republic whose owners have, since 1969, built one of the Caribbean's oldest, largest, and most popular tourism resort complexes, while simultaneously financing environmental and social programs to improve local livelihoods, ensure environmental protection, and address climate change. The final case study describes the CHENACT project, implemented by industry associations, whose mandate is to work with Caribbean hotels to improve energy efficiency, reduce utility costs, and mitigate greenhouse gas (GHG) emissions.

As stated, this volume focuses on coastal hotels, beaches, and shorelines. This focus is closely linked to a second volume on three auxiliary sectors—golf, local agriculture and cuisine, and airlines and airports—that are important components of the coastal tourism industry in the Caribbean. This second volume contains a final essay by Roger-Mark De Souza, "Challenges and Opportunities for the Caribbean," which serves as a conclusion for both these volumes. De Souza argues that "two key issues top the list of concerns and opportunities" for the Caribbean: "the impacts of climate change and imperative of responsible tourism." He goes on to summarize central themes from both volumes and to offer a five-point roadmap for sustainable coastal tourism and successful adaptation and mitigation to climate change in the Caribbean.

CHAPTER 2

Beach and Shoreline Protection

Overview—Protecting Shorelines from Impacts of Climate Change

Judi Clarke

Now more than ever, the Small Island Developing States (SIDS)[i] of the Caribbean need to find ways of reducing the vulnerability of their people and fragile tourism-reliant economies to the impacts of climate change. This is particularly important for beaches and shorelines, which are both the Caribbean's most important tourism assets and the front line in the battle to confront climate change. For decades, these beach and shoreline areas have been facing pressure from natural forces (such as wind, waves, tides, and currents) and human activities (beach sand removal and inappropriate tourism construction). The impacts of climate change, including sea level rise (SLR) and increasingly fierce and erratic storms, are already magnifying these pressures.

At the December 2015 United Nations Convention on Climate Change (UNFCCC COP21) in Paris,[1] governments struck a deal that commits countries to reducing their greenhouse gas emissions with

---

[i] There is a growing preference to refer to Small Island States as Large Ocean States because of their important role as ocean stewards, including addressing ocean-related climate change impacts.

the aim of limiting the further increase of global average temperature to 1.5°C. Although Caribbean and other small island states are already experiencing harsh impacts at current levels of warming, the 1.5°C target is seen as somewhat of a victory. Why? Two degrees of average warming would lead to SLR of some 2.7 m, which would spell the end for low-lying island countries. But despite the headway made at the Paris meeting, present-day SLR coupled with extreme weather events induced by climate change continues to pose one of the most immediate threats to Caribbean countries.

Finding workable solutions to protect beaches and shorelines as living, evolving ecosystems that also hold resorts and other built infrastructure is a complex balancing act. Many mistakes have been, and continue to be, made by those involved in protecting shorelines' natural and built environments, from property developers and owners, governments, and insurance companies, to social and natural scientists, engineers, and other technical experts. Really, it is essential that beach and shoreline protection be carried out in support of integrated sustainable development processes.

Coastal areas in the Caribbean, for all their appeal, are at the forefront of increasingly fierce and frequent tropical storms. Coastal ecosystems and the livelihoods that depend on them are also under increasing pressure. Beach erosion has removed public spaces where craft vendors ply their trade and has compromised landing sites for small fishing and tour

Image 2.0.1 Effects of coastal erosion in Barbados[2]

boats. Warmer sea surface temperatures have resulted in coral bleaching, making underwater sceneries less attractive to dive tourism.

Beach resorts and other coastal development projects are supposed to adhere to the legal coastal setback, the prescribed distance from a coastal feature such as the seaward line of vegetation, high tide mark, or dune crest (Fig. 2.1).

In the Caribbean, legal setbacks from the high tide mark range from 5 to 152 m depending on the country (Table 2.1).

However, in many locations, existing structures are allowed to be renovated and continue to operate within restricted zones. What's more, some developers intentionally violate the existing legal setback distance and they then either go unpunished or receive the penalty of a relatively modest fine. Such ill-conceived development puts natural and built systems—and people—at risk. Despite the growing realities of coastal

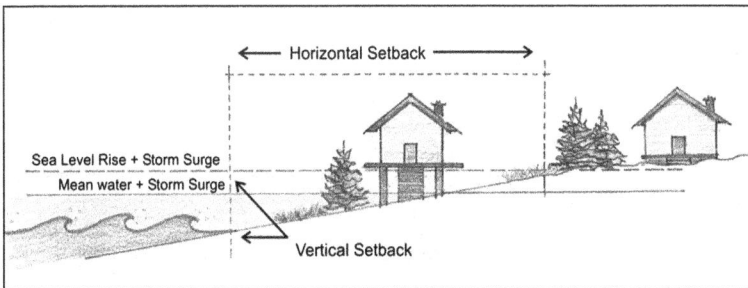

Figure 2.1 Horizontal and vertical coastal setback[3]

Table 2.1 Coastal setback distances for select Caribbean countries[4]

Country	Setback distance
Anguilla	15–91 m
Antigua and Barbuda	18–91 m
The Bahamas	5–15 m
Barbados	30 m/10 m cliff top
Belize	20 m
Cuba	40–80 m
Dominican Republic	60 m
Mexico	20 m
Nevis	18–152 m

vulnerability and loss, a degree of complacency continues to be the norm in much of the Caribbean. The pressures from climate change, coupled with destructive development, will, therefore, lead to certain demise of beaches and shorelines if appropriate interventions are not made . . . and soon.

Forecasts of Climate Change Impacts on Caribbean Coastal Tourism

From 2009 to mid-2016, CARIBSAVE[ii] (or INTASAVE Caribbean, a regional subsidiary of the international not-for-profit organization, INTASAVE) specialized in the delivery of climate-resilient and sustainable development solutions. CARIBSAVE worked throughout the Caribbean to evaluate the vulnerability of beaches and coastal infrastructure to SLR and storm surge at specific sites (identified as tourism hotspots) in a dozen participating countries.[iii] In a project conducted from 2010 through 2012, the organization used scenarios of 1 and 2 m SLR and of 50 and 100 m of beach erosion to calculate and assess the potential risks to beaches, critical tourism infrastructure, and major tourism resources, as well as to turtle nesting sites.

Results of these surveys indicate that 1 m SLR puts an estimated 38 percent of the major tourism properties on these islands at risk—and puts at risk over 70 percent of the tourism properties in Belize, Grenada, and Turks and Caicos. This 1 m scenario also predicts serious adverse impacts on airports, seaports, and major road networks. A 2 m SLR scenario puts at risk, on average, almost half of all tourism resorts in these dozen Caribbean countries. Indeed, with erosion damaging much of the tourism infrastructure, beaches will also essentially disappear.[5]

Another study conducted by the CARIBSAVE Partnership on CARICOM member states estimated the *cost* of damage to large resorts, as well as impacts on beaches, airports, and turtle nesting sites (Table 2.2).[6]

[ii] CARIBSAVE officially closed in July 2016, but the organization's website continues to function. For more information, see www.caribbean.intasave.org.

[iii] The dozen countries included were Anguilla, Antigua and Barbuda, The Bahamas, Barbados, Belize, Dominica, Grenada, Jamaica, Saint Lucia, St. Kitts and Nevis, St. Vincent and the Grenadines, and the Turks and Caicos Islands.

Table 2.2 Impacts of sea level rise on tourism in CARICOM member states[7]

Tourism asset	Effect of sea level rising by 1 m	Effect of sea level rising by 2 m
Large resorts	At least US$149 multi-million dollars' worth of tourism resorts damaged or lost	At least US$233 multi-million dollars' worth of tourism resorts damaged or lost
Beaches	Beach assets lost or greatly degraded at many tourist resorts	Beach assets lost or greatly degraded at most tourist resorts
Airports	Loss or damage to 21 CARICOM airports	Loss or damage to 31 CARICOM airports
Sea turtle nesting sites	Flooding of approximately a third of known nesting beaches	Flooding of approximately half of known nesting beaches

CARIBSAVE obtained high-resolution imagery for all the study sites, and this proved to be an essential tool for assessing vulnerability of infrastructure and settlements to future SLR. Such imagery also has the ability to identify individual properties, making it a very powerful risk communication tool. This information is proving valuable as well for discussions with policy makers and coastal communities on potential adaptation strategies.

Climatic changes and rising sea levels that are now being experienced in the Caribbean are in keeping with forecasts for the future. The Fifth Assessment Report of IPCC (Intergovernmental Panel on Climate Change) published in 2014 presents what scientists term an *intermediate low-emissions scenario* that forecasts changes between 2081 and 2100 (relative to 1986 and 2005) for the Caribbean. The predictions include:

- Decrease in average annual rainfall of about 5 to 6 percent
- 1.2°C to 2.3°C median annual increase in surface temperature
- SLR projections in the region of 0.5 to 0.6 m

If no meaningful action is taken, these projections will have dire implications for coastal tourism and related economic sectors, as well as for water and other natural resources. *If no meaningful action is taken.*

Responding to Climate Change:
What Are the Solutions to Protect Coastlines?

Vulnerable shorelines are often protected with hard structures, especially when an intervention is needed urgently. Ironically, however, these hard structures often exacerbate coastal erosion and adversely affect coastal ecosystems. Shorelines are living and changing places and therefore need protection that allows natural processes to take place.

There are four broad approaches to how coastal development, particularly related to tourism, could mitigate the current and projected impacts of climate change and SLR: (1) setbacks and retreat, (2) build back better, (3) hard engineering, and (4) soft engineering. In practice, not all of these approaches embrace the concept of a living shoreline, but each has its advantages. These approaches vary not only in their effectiveness but also in their acceptability to tourists (Case Study 2.2). Ultimately, most successful solutions incorporate a combination of approaches.

Setbacks and Retreat

One way of protecting coastal development from SLR and storm surge is to adhere to setback laws, where they exist, for new development. While this may be contrary to the main reason for developing in the coastal zone, that is to be close to the ocean, adhering to or even exceeding setbacks protects large investments in the long term. Some resorts have used creative and attractive landscaping on the seaside of coastal properties and this gives added protection. Some non-essential activities and amenities may also be placed in this area so that in the event of damage from storms, the facility can maintain essential services. However, for adaption to be successful, current setbacks must keep up with climate change and SLR projections.

Even in Caribbean islands where land for new development is scarce, there are opportunities to diversify the tourism product and shift focus away or retreat from the coast. The development of inland tourist accommodation facilities and activities should be seriously considered as worthwhile investments. Mountain retreats, cottages, or historic villas nestled amongst trees can provide an equally satisfying experience for

many visitors. Every Caribbean country has unique cultural, gastronomi-
cal, and historic offerings that can be exploited far more than they are
currently—and on small islands, the beach is never far away.

There is a paucity of examples in the Caribbean of inland tourism
development, including Belmont Estate in Grenada, Kittitian Hill Resort
in St. Kitts, and Sugar Ridge in Antigua (Case Study 3.2). However,
for most Caribbean island states, inland retreat, in the sense of shifting
tourism infrastructure away from coastal areas, may not be a feasible
option. Not only are there often few attractive alternatives, but it is also
an unpopular strategy as long as coastal areas still fetch prime dollar for
tourism development. As the case study on vacation homes along North
Carolina's Outer Banks demonstrates, the majority of homeowners do
not believe that climate change is going to negatively impact their beach
or property values (Case Study 2.1).

Build Back Better

After damage or destruction from storm events, tourism facilities should
build back to better withstand future events. Whilst the science isn't
perfect, there is sufficient information available to inform engineering and
construction methods with climate change considerations. Developers
should be aware of existing techniques to build infrastructure along
coastal fringes that better withstands high winds, excessive rainfall, and
storm surges predicted as a result of climate change. Secondary impacts
can also cause significant damage. For example, high winds can fell trees
onto buildings or turn large, otherwise-immobile objects into airborne
projectiles, while erosive wave action can undermine foundations that
support coastal infrastructure.

Because *build back better* information doesn't always get into the right
hands, scientists and governments should work together in order to increase
awareness and capacity amongst engineers, planners, policy makers, and
the users of coastal resources. Caution must also be raised against trade-
offs that favor building structures with an eye on short-term economic
savings that inevitably result in larger cumulative costs over time.

In August 2015, Tropical Storm Erika caused extensive infrastructure
damage in Dominica, including destroying one well known eco-lodge.

The government commissioned Rapid Assessment[8] following the storm revealed that a lot of relatively new infrastructure had failed to survive because of poor design and/or quality of construction. Now that Dominica has entered a post-disaster reconstruction phase, there is great potential to reassess the most appropriate design and construction methods that will ultimately contribute to long-term resilience. In other words, they have the opportunity to build back better.

Hard Engineering

To date, most efforts to stabilize beaches and shorelines have involved either *hard* or *soft* engineering techniques. What is known as *hard engineering* can provide immediate protection and other benefits if carried out sensibly. There are many examples of beachfront property owners constructing walls or placing boulders as protection from the sea. However, what this often does is promote further erosion of the existing beach because these structures insufficiently account for the complex interplay of wave and sediment movements. These movements effectively govern when, where, and how much sand is moved or deposited along different points of a continuous near shore zone.

But not all hard engineering experiments have been bad; some have proven successful. Take, for instance, the South Coast Boardwalk in Barbados. This 1.6 km stretch of hard engineered walkway was designed as the solution to a narrowing beach. It has given immediate protection from storm surges to the private homes, hotels, restaurants, and bars in the area, while locals and tourists enjoy the Boardwalk for recreational activities.

Importantly, the Boardwalk has been designed to withstand strong storms. It consists of a concrete superstructure with sacrificial timber decking that may be lost during major storms. This successful project also includes the nourishment of the areas between five main headlands, which allows continued natural processes of sediment transport and beach enrichment.[9]

In addition, other coastal areas are effectively protected by offshore breakwaters that reduce the wave energy at a distance off shore. Depending on the materials used, these can also create a habitat for fish

Image 2.0.3 An example of hard engineering that was unable to prevent further beach erosion in Antigua[10]

Image 2.0.4 Many people use the Boardwalk for social and recreational activities throughout the day[11]

and coral. One such example, also found in Barbados, is the Rockley Beach breakwater. It was constructed in 1994 as part of a pilot project to investigate its potential for beach stabilization. This 150-m-long submerged crest breakwater is located in approximately 5 m of water and has functioned beautifully, making Rockley Beach (commonly known as Accra Beach for its proximity to the hotel of the same name) the most popular beach on the south coast.

The breakwater has also served as an artificial reef supporting a variety of benthic organisms, including coral and algae that live on or just above the seafloor. This provides food for reef fish, which in turn provide food for the larger predators such as the barracuda.[12]

Soft Engineering

Soft engineering approaches are also being used to protect living shorelines. One technique, known as Ecosystem-based Adaptation (EbA), uses biodiversity as part of an overall adaptation strategy to help communities cope with the negative effects of climate change. Mangroves and other estuarine systems, sea grass beds, and coral reefs can provide substantial protection against destructive waves by absorbing or dampening energy from waves as they approach the shore. Coral reefs also provide sediment that helps to form beaches and dunes, which add another layer of shoreline protection.

These natural buffers in healthy, stable conditions have great potential to minimize the impacts from storm surges and other high-energy wave events, reducing damage along the coastline and also reducing the risk and extent of coastal flooding. A number of Caribbean island shorelines benefit from the presence of one or more of these natural assets, but in particular, the islands of Grenada, Saint Lucia, Jamaica, St. Vincent and the Grenadines, and The Bahamas have been recognized for their suitability to employ or expand on EbA approaches.[13]

EbA can therefore be considered a *no-regrets* climate change adaptation strategy in that it also provides many other benefits to communities, for example through the maintenance and enhancement of ecosystem services such as clean water and food.[14] Healthy, well-functioning ecosystems enhance natural resilience to the adverse impacts of climate change and reduce the vulnerability of people[15] thereby supporting sustainable development. EbA is therefore increasingly recognized as a feasible adaptation strategy. However, because effective EbA approaches take time to work, shoreline protection is often sought first through engineering structures. For proponents of such an engineered approach, the priority is typically to first protect man-made coastal capital, then pay attention to the ecosystems. But really, the two solutions should work in tandem,

Image 2.0.5 Mangrove replanting in Tortola acts as a wave and erosion buffer along the coastline[16]

providing, let's say, a wide beach made safe from the onslaught of waves by submerged breakwaters, plus vibrant, living reefs in front of or close to the same property.

Conclusions

Weather-related events have been causing damage and destruction to lives and livelihoods in coastal areas in the Caribbean, and climate change is only making matters worse. Caribbean coastlines face a continuous threat from climate variability and change, and coastline protection is a necessity for social and economic security in many of these countries. This fact is not lost on Caribbean governments, and some countries have embarked upon coastline protection interventions—albeit with varied levels of success.

Hard and soft engineering approaches have perhaps been deemed most feasible for the Caribbean, largely because retreat options— moving away from the coast—are viewed as bringing less economic return than higher-value coastal real estate developments. In addition, higher resourced projects, which incorporate hard-engineering com- ponents, are considered to have a greater return on investment than ecosystem-based solutions. However, in most cases, not enough time has passed to allow for maturity and a realization of benefits from soft engineering options like mangrove rehabilitation and coral restoration projects.

Barbados stands out as a Caribbean leader in integrated coastal zone management. The Government of Barbados has long recognized that any threat to its coastal and marine environment would have devastating consequences, given the island's economic dependence on coastal tourism. The Coastal Zone Management Unit (CZMU) was created in 1996 to establish regulations and educate the Barbadian population about coastal management. Additionally, the Barbados Physical Development Plan (amended in 2003 and currently undergoing another revision) guides development on the island to ensure a multidisciplinary approach to planning in collaboration with various government agencies. As a result, the regulatory body for planning and the Coastal Zone Management Unit work together to ensure that development in the coastal zone does not compromise the coastal environment.

The development potential of most Caribbean countries is constrained by a lack of sufficient financial and technical resources to pursue a sustainable coastal protection agenda. The extent of input that is required for long-term, high-impact protection unfortunately goes beyond the capacity of many Caribbean states. Due to limited financial resources, Caribbean countries should prioritize using *no regrets* solutions that address present-day sustainable development needs as well as support adaptation to future climate changes. Some of these include:

- Integration of SLR, storm surge, and flooding risks into national development plans to ensure that consideration is given to climate change in future development and construction. Development plans can list classes of development for which an environmental impact assessment (EIA) that incorporates climate change is required. The EIA should therefore provide for enforceability, addressing the coastal impacts of climate change through setback requirements and property protection measures.

- Develop a program to support economic diversification in coastal areas through additional opportunities to increase resilience in the face of uncertainty and change. Options include craft production, small-scale tourism, aquaculture, heritage tours, coral gardening/ farming, and coral rehabilitation (Case Study 2.3). Livelihoods combining activities that vary in their climate response and sensitivity will be more adaptable to climate change.
- Establish a link between insurance policies to account for the long-term risks of SLR, more intense storms, flood risks, and construction quality to encourage landowners to assess options, including possible relocation. Insurance incentives are the most efficient market-based tools for ensuring that the design of built structures incorporates future climate risks. These incentives would include lower deductibles and premiums for those who invest in adaptation measures and retrofits.
- Help support reef resilience and recovery by addressing stressors on reefs that occur locally such as those from marine vessels and from surface run-off.

Notes

1. Mairi Dupar, Kiran Sura, and Sam Bickersteth. (2015). "OPINION: COP21 Draws to Strong End with Adoption of 1.5 Degree Goal," Climate and Development Knowledge Network (CDKN). http://cdkn.org/2015/12/cop21-outcome/?loclang=en_gb
2. Image Source: CARIBSAVE.
3. Colleen Mercer Clarke and John D. Clarke. (2012). *Managing Change: A Discussion of the Application of Land Use Planning and Development Instruments Over Time and Space*. Working Paper of the C-CHANGE Project. Ottawa, Ontario.
4. Adapted from Murray C. Simpson, Colleen Mercer Clarke, John D. Clarke, Daniel Scott, and Alexander Clarke. (2012). *Coastal Setbacks in Latin America and the Caribbean: Final Report*. A study of

emerging issues and trends that inform guidelines for coastal planning and development.Inter-American Development Bank.

5. Murray C. Simpson, J.F. Clarke, D.J. Scott, M. New, A. Karmalkar,
O.J. Day, M. Taylor, S. Gössling, M. Wilson, D. Chadee, N. Fields,
H. Stager, R. Waithe, A. Stewart, J. Georges, R. Sim, N. Hutchinson,
M. Rutty, L. Matthews, and S. Charles. (2012). *CARIBSAVE Climate
Change Risk Atlas*. Barbados: DFID, AusAID, and The CARIBSAVE
Partnership: Barbados, West Indies.

6. Murray C. Simpson, D.J. Scott, M. Harrison, N. Silver, E. O'Keeffe,
S. Harrison, M. Taylor, R. Sim, G. Lizcano, M. Wilson, M. Rutty,
H. Stager, J. Oldham, M. New, J. Clarke, O.J. Day, N. Fields,
J. Georges, R. Waithe, and P. McSharry. (2010a). *Quantification and
Magnitude of Losses and Damages Resulting from the Impacts of Climate
Change: Modelling the Transformational Impacts and Costs of Sea Level
Rise in the Caribbean*. Barbados: United Nations Development
Program (UNDP).

7. Murray C. Simpson, D.J. Scott, M. Harrison, N. Silver, E. O'Keeffe,
S. Harrison, M. Taylor, R. Sim, G. Lizcano, M. Wilson, M. Rutty,
H. Stager, J. Oldham, M. New, J. Clarke, O.J. Day, N. Fields,
J. Georges, R. Waithe, and P. McSharry. (2010a).

8. Government of the Commonwealth of Dominica. (August 27,
2015). *Rapid Damage and Impact Assessment: Tropical Storm Erika*.

9. Baird. (2015). "Beach Restoration and Boardwalk." http://www
.baird.com/what-we-do/project/beach-restoration-and-boardwalk.

10. Image Source: CARIBSAVE.

11. Image Source: CARIBSAVE. (2012).

12. Coastal Zone Management Unit (CZMU). (2015). *Protected Marine
Areas: Folkestone Park and Marine Reserve*. http://www.coastal.gov
.bb/pageselect.cfm?page=17.

13. Bruno Chatenoux and Alexander Wolf. (2013). *Ecosystem-based
Approaches for Climate Change Adaptation in Caribbean SIDS
(Report)*. Switzerland and Germany: UNEP/GRID-Geneva and
ZMT Leibniz Center for Tropical Marine Biology.

14. United Nations Environment Programme (UNEP). (2015a).
Climate Change Adaptation: Building Resilience of Ecosystems for

Adaptation.   http://www.unep.org/climatechange/adaptation/EbA
/tabid/29583/Default.aspx.

15. United Nations Environment Programme (UNEP). (2015a).

16. Image Source: Island Resources Foundation. (2007).

Case Study 2.1

Climate and Weather Impacts on Tourism and Vacation Homes in Coastal North Carolina

by Huili Hao, Patrick Long, and Scott Curtis

The coastal areas of the United States are home to 50 percent of the nation's total population—and the more attractive coastal counties and communities are typically heavily affected by tourism and second home development. The IPCC has indicated that vulnerabilities of industries, infrastructures, settlements, and society to climate change are generally greater in coastal communities and certain other high-risk areas.[1] An amenity-rich coastal tourism destination, one with dependence upon a second home vacation economy, will most certainly be affected by climate change. Tourism is highly sensitive to climate changes, which, in turn, can directly affect the attractiveness of destinations to current and future property owners and disturb local economies by impacting investments in the construction and maintenance of second homes.

As popular tourism destinations evolve from providing general tourism products and services to also becoming desirable second home destinations, relevant planning, policy, and management issues must be addressed. Less analysis has been done to date regarding a number of issues surrounding how second homeowners and permanent residents perceive the effects of climate and weather on location decisions and recreational pursuits.[2] In an effort to analyze these issues, East Carolina University's Center for Sustainability conducted a study in 2011 to assess the perceptions of full-time residents ($n = 696$) and second home property owners ($n = 785$) on the impacts of tourism and second home development in three North Carolina coastal counties. In addition, these property owners were asked to determine the manner and extent to which climate impacts are likely to affect their future property values and recreational decisions.

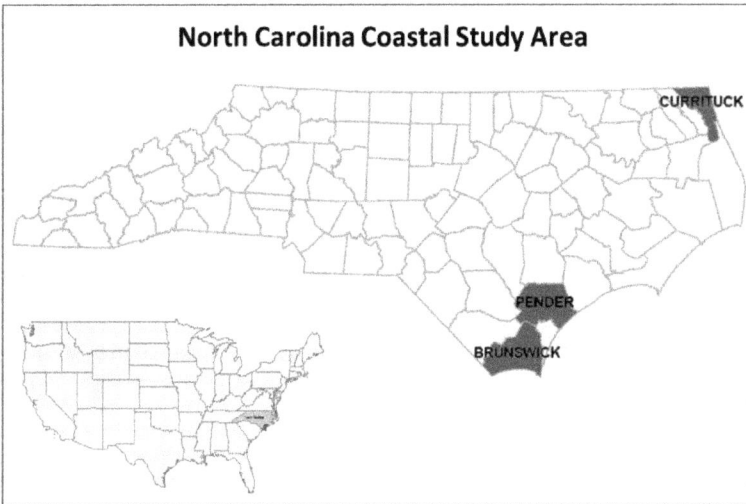

Figure 2.2 Study Area: Currituck, Pender, and Brunswick Counties, North Carolina[3]

North Carolina Study Area

The study selected three coastal counties—Brunswick, Currituck, and Pender—based upon their location, desirability as a tourist destination, and high prevalence of second homes (Fig. 2.2).

With tourism being a major economic driver of these counties and with almost 40 percent of the housing stock being second homes,[4] these are locales where the advantages and disadvantages of tourism are regularly debated. Debates are known to include tourists, public policy makers, business owners and operators, full-time residents, and second home property owners.

The North Carolina Department of Commerce, Division of Tourism, Film and Sports Development reported that in 2013 domestic tourism generated US$692.47 million of economic impact in these counties with 7,290 jobs directly attributable to tourism.[5] Additionally, tourism in these counties resulted in some US$125 million in payroll and over US$70 million in state and local tax revenue.[6]

Impacts of Climate and Weather on Property Ownership

The geographic information system (GIS) Tax Records of each county provided a list of housing stock from which we selected a sample of both resident and second home property owners. The sample includes 7,192 second home property owners and 7,395 full-time/permanent property owners. Second home property owners were identified as those who own property in the study area but have their property tax bills sent to another address. We received 1,481 useable, completed questionnaires (696 from permanent resident and 785 from vacation homeowners). This equals a response rate of about 9 percent.

Study participants were asked to indicate their level of agreement with how climate and weather affects their ownership of property in their county (Fig. 2.3).

The majority of the homeowners (60 percent full time and 79 percent second home property owners) agreed or strongly agreed that "weather and climate conditions were important in deciding to own property in the county." Less than 10 percent of the property owners agreed that "weather conditions have changed enough in the county" that they "would not

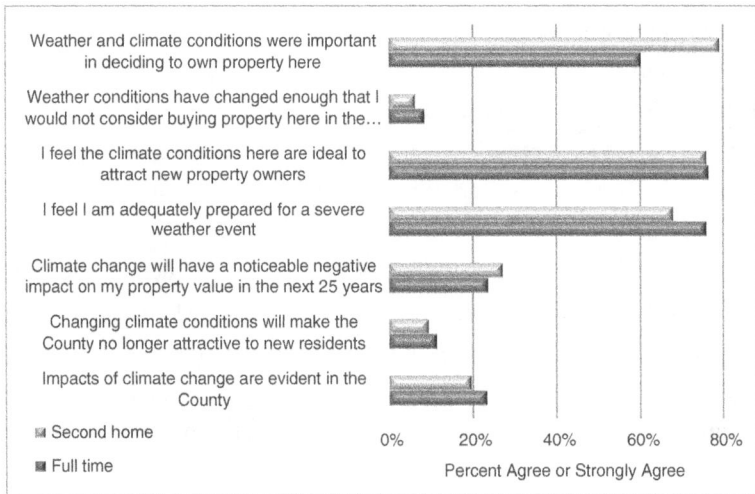

Figure 2.3 Attitudes of full-time residents and second home property owners toward how weather and climate affect property ownership[7]

consider buying property" there in the future. Further, over 65 percent of the homeowners agreed that they were "adequately prepared for a severe weather event (such as hurricanes, floods, and heavy rains)" and felt that "climate conditions here are ideal to attract new property owners."

Interestingly, when asked specifically about climate change, only about 20 to 25 percent agreed with the statement that "impacts of climate change are evident in the county." Further, less than 30 percent of the property owners (24 percent full-time residents and 27 percent second homeowners) agreed on the statement that "climate change will have a noticeable negative impact on my property value in the next 25 years." Even fewer—15 percent or less—of both categories said that "changing climate conditions will make the county no longer attractive to new residents." In sum, when asked directly about the impacts of climate change, neither category of homeowner appeared terribly worried.

Climate Change and Future Property Values

Participants were further asked to express their views about how specific climate change factors will affect their future property values (Fig. 2.4).

More than 50 percent of second home property owners agreed that the number and intensity of coastal storms, SLR, and coastal flooding, as well as availability of freshwater, are the factors that would affect their

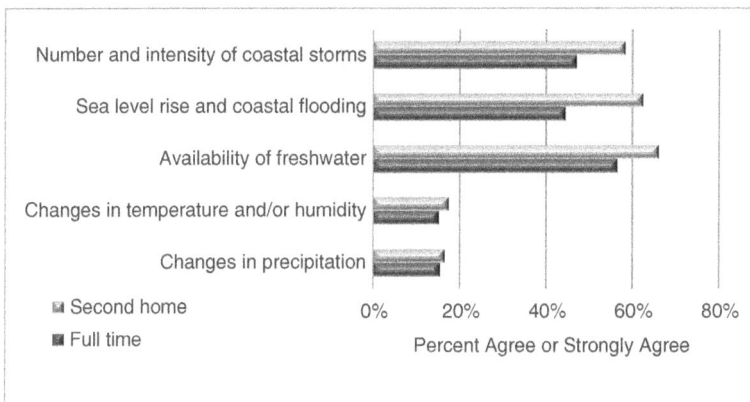

Figure 2.4 Attitudes of full-time residents and second home property owners toward how climate changes will affect property value[8]

future property values. In contrast, less than 50 percent of the full-time residents indicated that these same factors would affect their future property values. For both categories of homeowners less than 20 percent said that more minor weather changes—in precipitation, temperature, and/or humidity—would impact property values.

Weather Factors in Making Personal Recreational Decisions

Participants were asked to indicate the extent to which they consider weather factors (temperature, humidity, wind, and precipitation) when making personal recreational decisions (Fig. 2.5).

More than 50 percent of the homeowners indicated that precipitation and temperature affected their personal recreational decisions. In addition, less than half—some 40 percent of full-time resident property owners and only 30 percent of second homeowners—said "wind" and "humidity" affected their personal recreational decisions.

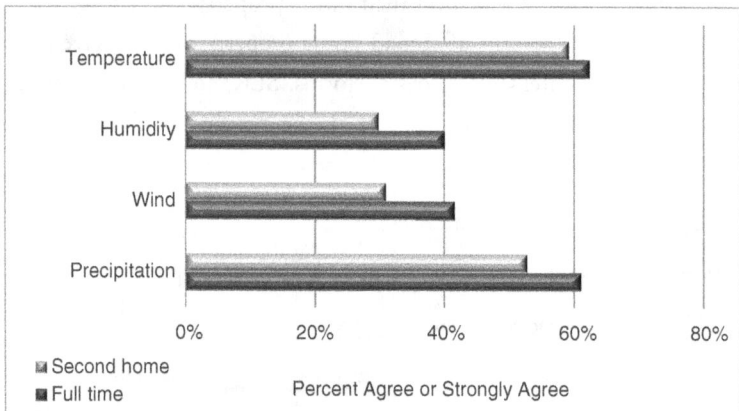

Figure 2.5 Attitudes of full-time residents and second home property owners toward how weather variables affect personal recreational decisions[9]

Summary and Policy Implications

The survey results revealed some significant differences between residents and second home property owners. Decisions to buy property in coastal

North Carolina are more dependent on weather for second or vacation homeowners than for permanent residents (20 percent difference). One explanation for this difference is that permanent residents may move to the area because of employment or other necessitating factors. Second home property owners are also more concerned about how their investment will withstand hazards such as coastal storms and flooding, which may be climate change induced. Permanent residents may also have more experience with these hazards and may have less capability of moving, and thus may not perceive these hazards as such a threat. Further, second homes are generally closer to the beach and will receive the brunt of these oceanic hazards. When our survey asked second homeowners "why did you buy your second home property in the county?," more than 84 percent of the respondents indicated close proximity to the beach was the primary reason. Freshwater may also become scarcer near the beach due to SLR and groundwater salinization.

It is interesting to note that permanent residents use wind and humidity factors when making personal recreational decisions more than do second home property owners. This result is consistent with previous research in coastal North Carolina, which found that local beach-goers were more sensitive to wind than non-locals. We attribute this to locals having a greater appreciation of micro-climates (e.g., land sea breeze) and their effects on recreational activities.

As the survey finds, weather and climate conditions can significantly affect tourism, recreational activities, and property ownership and value in a region. These findings are important when formulating policies and can also help set the stage for communication and education activities with the different property owner groups. However, it is interesting to note that *neither group is particularly concerned when asked directly about climate change*. All residents with financial investment at the beach may be biased against recognizing climate change ("heads buried in the sand"), when, in fact, observational evidence and models overwhelmingly point to an acceleration of SLR in coastal North Carolina.[10]

In contrast, when both groups were asked about increasing severity of specific climate change related factors—the number and intensity of coastal storms, SLR, and coastal flooding, as well as availability of freshwater—50 percent or more of each group said these factors would affect their future property values. This may reflect the ongoing political debate in North Carolina over SLR projections and the validity of the concept of climate change.[11] Future work must focus on how to bridge this gap between denial and reality if tourism is to be a sustainable option near beaches and coastlines in the United States, the Caribbean, and elsewhere.

Notes

1. C.B. Field, V.R. Barros, D.J. Dokken, K.J. Mach, M.D. Mastrandrea, T.E. Bilir, M. Chatterjee, K.L. Ebi, Y.O. Estrada, R.C. Genova, B. Girma, E.S. Kissel, A.N. Levy, S. MacCracken, P.R. Mastrandrea, and L.L. White (eds.), IPCC. (2014). "Climate Change 2014: Impacts, Adaptation, and Vulnerability. Part A: Global and Sectoral Aspects." *Contribution of Working Group II to the Fifth Assessment Report of the Intergovernmental Panel on Climate Change.* Cambridge, UK: Cambridge University Press. p. 1132.

2. Scott Curtis, Jennifer Arrigo, Patrick Long, and Ryan Covington. (2009). *Climate, Weather, and Tourism: Bridging Science and Practice.* East Carolina University Press. p. 14.

3. Figure Source: Huili Hao, Patrick Long, Whitney Knollenberg, Craig Landry, and Tom Crawford. (2010–2012). "Tourism Impacts and Second Home Development in Coastal Counties: A Sustainable Approach." https://www.ecu.edu/cs-cet/sustainability/tourism/upload/Study-Report-Brunswick-County.pdf. This project is funded by North Carolina Sea Grant.

4. Huili Hao, Patrick Long, Whitney Knollenberg, Craig Landry, and Tom Crawford. (2010–2012).

5. U.S. Travel Association. (September 2014). "The Economic Impact of Travel on North Carolina Counties 2013, A Study Prepared for the North Carolina Division of Tourism, Film and Sports Development". Washington, DC: U.S. Travel Association. https://www.nccommerce.com/LinkClick.aspx?fileticket=2vuxET_5uHA%3D&tabid=1586&mid=4665

6. Ryan Covington, Jennifer Arrigo, Scott Curtis, Patrick Long, and Derek H. Alderman. (2009-2010). "Tourists' Climate Perceptions:

A Survey of Preferences and Sensitivities in North Carolina's Outer Banks." *The North Carolina Geographer,* 17. pp. 38–53.

7. Figure Source: Huili Hao, Patrick Long, Whitney Knollenberg, Craig Landry, and Tom Crawford. (2010–2012).

8. Figure Source: Huili Hao, Patrick Long, Whitney Knollenberg, Craig Landry, and Tom Crawford. (2010–2012).

9. Figure Source: Huili Hao, Patrick Long, Whitney Knollenberg, Craig Landry, and Tom Crawford. (2010–2012).

10. Stanley R. Riggs, Stephen J. Culver, Dorothea V. Ames, David J. Mallinson, D. Reid Corbett, and J.P. Walsh. (2008). "North Carolina's Coast in Crisis: A Vision for the Future," East Carolina University Press. p. 26.

11. Stanley R. Riggs, Stephen J. Culver, Dorothea V. Ames, David J. Mallinson, D. Reid Corbett. and J.P. Walsh. (2008). p. 26; Lori Montgomery. (June 24, 2014). "On N.C.'s Outer Banks, Scary Climate-Change Predictions Prompt a Change of Forecast," *Washington Post.*

Case Study 2.2

Travelers' Response to Beach Loss and Shoreline Protection Measures

by Michelle Rutty

In the Caribbean, tourism has been built around images of idyllic, pristine, white sand beaches. In order to maintain a strong international tourism clientele, coastal resorts have sought to uphold a natural beach aesthetic, with undisrupted ocean views and unhindered access to beach areas.[1] Since the 1990s, however, research has begun to outline the potential impacts of climate change for the future of coastal tourism, including the loss of high-value beaches and the increased need for shoreline protection.[2]

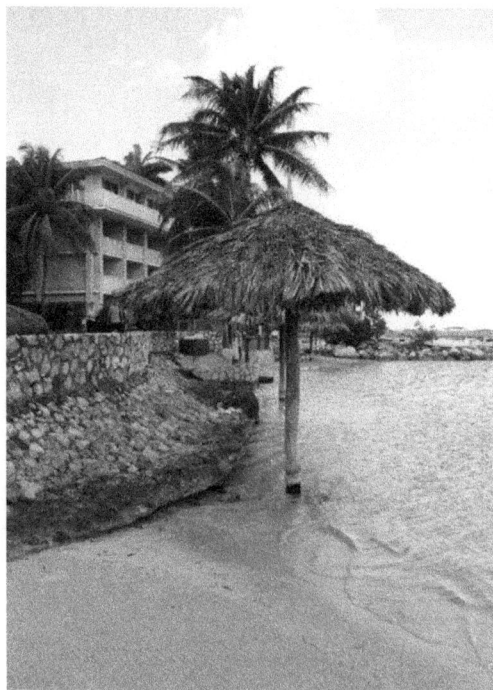

Image 2.2.1 Beach loss and shoreline protection in Montego Bay, Jamaica[3]

An estimated 29 percent of resort properties in the Caribbean are projected to be either partially or fully inundated as a result of climate change related SLR, with an additional 49 to 60 percent of resort properties at risk of beach erosion damage.[4] For some islands, Anguilla, Belize, British Virgin Islands, Saint Kitts and Nevis, Turks and Caicos, the loss of coastal resorts is projected to be well over 50 percent, not to mention many resorts would experience significant beach area loss prior to property loss.[5]

Scientists and engineers have experimented with various methods to avoid or reduce these negative impacts. These methods vary not only in their effectiveness, but also in their acceptability to tourists.

Shoreline Protection Techniques

One of the most widespread techniques has been the use of hard engineered coastal protection measures including building structures such as *groynes*, which are structures that extend perpendicular from the shore into the water, and *sea walls*, structures that parallel the shoreline. However, in addition to the high capital investment and maintenance costs, these protection strategies have proved only partially effective in preventing beach erosion, as hard engineering measures can increase erosion on down drift beaches and promote shoreline scouring under the sea wall.[6] In addition, hard protection measures can reduce the attractiveness of coastal resorts and beaches to tourists, putting the overall appeal—and profitability—of the destination at risk.

An alternative method, beach nourishment or sand replenishment can maintain the natural beach aesthetic and may subsequently result in little or no decline in tourism demand.[7] This shoreline protection strategy involves taking sediment from an outside source and putting it either directly on the eroding beach or underwater in mounds or dunes in order to push the shoreline seaward. However, since this method does not remove the physical forces that cause erosion, it is only a temporary solution that often requires repeated—and costly—replenishment.[8] For example, in a major restoration project in Cancun, Mexico, dredged sand was spread along a seven-mile stretch of beach between 40 and 70 m wide, costing an estimated US$70 million in 2009.[9] Just one year later,

6 to 8 percent of this new sand had already washed away, even without any major storms.[i10]

There is also evidence that beach replenishment projects may lead to maladaptation because they may encourage further development along the coastline, as evidenced in Miami and North Carolina, resulting in an ever-increasing need for shoreline protection measures.[11] A third coastal protection strategy includes the restoration and rehabilitation of mangroves, which provide a natural barrier against currents, waves, and storms and thereby help to absorb and dissipate tidal force. However, the buffering capacity of mangroves is highly variable and depends on tree density, stem and root diameter, shoreline elevation and slope, the presence of dunes and other vegetation, as well as the frequency, size, and duration of the tidal force.[12] The success of this approach is also directly linked to ecosystem health because mangroves themselves can be damaged by waves. This requires a balance between *resilience*, meaning the ability to recover from a disturbance and *vulnerability*, meaning the susceptibility to be adversely affected, which is further threatened by the concomitant effects of climate change such as increased temperatures, altered precipitation patterns, increased storm frequency, and SLR.[13] From a tourist point of view, mangroves are unlikely to be —at least without education and understanding—an attractive alternative because similar to hard engineering structures, mangroves inhibit direct access to and views of the beach.

A fourth protection measure is managed retreat and coastal setback. This determines the minimum distance (horizontal setback) or elevation (vertical setback) to a coastal feature such as high tide water mark, seaward line of vegetation, or dune crest, within which development is prohibited.[14] By allowing the sea to naturally move inland, setbacks retain the natural beach aesthetic and direct access, while minimizing property damage due to coastal flooding and erosion. Coastal setbacks are clearly far easier to do at the construction stage, while managed retreat of existing resorts is costly. And for many Caribbean destinations, retreat is not possible because land is not available, particularly in highly developed areas.

---

[i] Unfortunately, a literature review found no reports or studies of what has happened since 2010.

Image 2.2.2 Abandoned tourism infrastructure along the coastline of Barbados[15]

Or it may be that setback is difficult because of planning and legal issues, including considerations for property loss, heritage rights, and high compensation costs.[16] Yet if a coastal resort cannot be setback, the alternative is to leave the structure damaged and eventually abandoned, thereby degrading the overall aesthetics of the coastline.

Importance of Understanding Travelers' Perceptions

In recent years, there have been significant advances in climate change science research in the Caribbean,[17] yet there have been remarkably few studies that have examined how travelers will respond to climate change impacts and adaptation, both regionally and globally.[18] This is alarming given that tourists have the greatest capacity to adapt to climate change.[19] Unlike most tourism businesses, which have substantial capital investments in immobile infrastructure such as hotels and resorts, restaurants, golf courses, marines, shopping facilities, cruise ports, and airports, tourists can easily alter the destination, timing, and frequency of their holiday, even at a very short notice.[20]

Beach tourism destinations in the Caribbean are in a state of continual competition. This includes competition with adjacent beaches on the same island, beaches on neighboring islands, as well as with international beach destinations. With such high competition, tourism demand for beach holidays depends on a balance between the perceived quality of the beach and the price of the trip.[21] Understanding travelers' perceptions and responses to beach loss and shoreline protection strategies is therefore essential to anticipate future shifts in tourism demand and the overall competitiveness of Caribbean tourism businesses and destinations.[22]

Tourist Response to Beach Loss

The first study to examine travelers' responses to future scenarios of SLR and beach loss was conducted along the German coasts of the North and Baltic Seas in the late 1990s. Study participants were given a scenario describing negative climate change effects, including higher humidity, monsoon-like rainfall, far-reaching ecological changes, and permanent danger of storms during spring and fall, calumniating in real storm tides as the sea level continues to rise. [23] The results found that tourists would be "less eager" to travel to the German coast in the future, even where possible shoreline protection measures such as resort and other infrastructure setbacks were implemented. However, it is unclear to what degree tourists were deterred by the relocation of infrastructure inland versus the described changes in climate. In a similar study in 2010 examining the UK coastline, beach loss resulted in only a slight decrease in tourism demand of <1 percent, although the change scenarios presented were relatively small, for example, <5 percent loss on beaches with widths of <250 m.[24] Given the forecast, such minor beach loss is not applicable for the majority of coastal properties in the Caribbean.

To date, there has only been one study of visitor attitudes in the Caribbean—and it was published in 2005. According to the study, of the tourists surveyed in Barbados, 77 percent indicated that they would not be willing to return to the island for the same price under a scenario where the beaches largely disappeared.[25] Even in Bonaire, which is predominantly a dive tourism destination and hence beaches are not the primary tourism asset, almost half (43 percent) of the respondents indicated they would not return if the beaches on the island disappeared.[26]

Only a handful of studies have attempted to translate potential demand changes from beach loss into economic losses for a destination. In the coastal US state of North Carolina, a conservative projection of 46 cm rise in sea level by 2080 (note many scientific projections exceed 1 m)[27] was estimated to result in a US$3.5 billion loss in recreational benefits from reduced opportunities for beach trips. This SLR would also place at risk residential properties totaling US$1.2 billion in value. A large proportion of these are vacation homes and with their loss, tourism spending would decline even further than what was estimated.[28]

Tourist Response to Shoreline Protection

Even fewer studies have considered traveler perceptions, experiences, and attitudes toward beach and shoreline protection designed to counter climate change impacts. It is relatively unclear how tourists perceive and respond to engineering measures to protect coastal shorelines, including travelers' subjective view toward these adaptive strategies. The only study to explore this issue was conducted on the Caribbean coast in Playacar, Mexico.[29] Tourists were interviewed in person and also online comments were reviewed regarding their trip experiences with the existing beach erosion and restoration attempts of using large geotextile bags as erosion control devices. *Geotextile technology* is a recent economical alternative that transforms traditional hard engineering structures by using soft materials, such as flexible fabric bags filled with sand. Its success at coastal protection is heavily dependent on the placement, size, and maintenance of the bags.[30]

The study found that the visitor responses to the protective strategy varied. Some enjoyed the additional recreational opportunities provided by the geotextile bags in the water because swimmers could jump off the structures and use them as shelter from waves or as sunbathing platforms. Others, however, felt deceived, indicating that they had expected the extensive and pristine beaches depicted in marketing brochures and not the "ugly," "artificial" sandbags, which they also viewed as dangerous because they are slippery, causing people to fall off and sometimes hurt themselves. Interestingly, those tourists that were aware of the beach protection measures prior to traveling from reading online reviews on

Image 2.2.3 Geotextile bags[31]

TripAdvisor were unanimous in stating that the geotextile bags were aesthetically unpleasant, but they were also accepting, viewing the bags as a necessary effort to combat Mother Nature or climate change. It remains unclear whether the uninformed tourists would have been deterred from booking their holiday in Playacar had they known beforehand about the beach erosion and geotextile bags, or whether having this knowledge would prove an important factor enabling tourists to be more accepting of coastal protection measures.

While the North Carolina studies mentioned above look at the economic losses from climate change, to date, just one study has estimated the economic implications of decreased tourism demand resulting from shoreline protection strategies. Using a hedonic pricing method,[ii] it was estimated that the diminished shoreline aesthetics from the proposed construction of coastal levies in the town of Schleswig-Holstein in northern Germany would lead to an estimated loss of €1.2 million per year from lost accommodation revenues.[32] However, if beach nourishment was used to protect the shoreline, it was estimated that there would be no loss in revenue. While this strategy would protect tourism demand, the

---

[ii] A model identifying price factors according to the premise that price is determined both by internal characteristics of the item being sold and external factors affecting it.

estimated cost was considerable. Using the neighboring coastal district of Westerland as a comparable, beach nourishment would be required approximately every six years at a cost of €3.6 million on each occasion.[33]

Moving Forward

To date, little consideration has been given to the role of tourist perceptions to not only climate change, but also climate change adaptation strategies. It is disconcerting that travelers' perceptions, experiences, and attitudes toward beach loss and shoreline protection have yet to receive sufficient consideration given the inherent importance of tourism demand in the Caribbean. While available studies are few, they underscore that demand for particular beach destinations, including price structures for accommodation, may decrease in the future as a result of climate change related SLR and beach erosion.

As destinations seek to deal with climate change through adaptations designed to lessen potential impacts, it is imperative that we account for how travelers may respond to adaptation strategies. While beach nourishment may maintain tourism demand, it is a temporary measure that may be cost prohibitive for many island destinations in the Caribbean. On the other hand, hard engineered structures may be a necessary course of action to protect some tourism assets such as airports and cruise ship terminals, but may fail to be an effective strategy for coastal resort properties that rely on a natural beach aesthetic as their main attraction.[34] Further, hard engineered structures are far from fool proof. They disrupt normal patterns of wind, wave, and current movement, which in turn impact sediment exchange, including the supply, deposition, and grain size. This can cause erosion on adjacent beaches, resulting in declining tourism demand for these beaches, and perhaps the entire destination.

Devising shoreline protection measures that are accepted by tourists is increasingly important with the advent of social media. Websites such as TripAdvisor host over 30 million customer reviews a month, providing a forum where travelers can share real-time photos and comments that can directly influence the travel decisions of potential tourists worldwide. As such, industry marketing of pristine beaches is increasingly challenged.[35] Tourist reaction on social media to the sargassum epidemic in the

Caribbean underscores this point and raises further questions about travelers' willingness to visit a beach destination that uses shoreline protection measures that are deemed to be unattractive and undesirable. As the study of Playacar indicates, it is possible that if properly informed about climate change and efforts to decrease its impacts on beaches and shorelines, tourists may be more accepting of proactive strategies. Collectively, the preceding evidence underscores that much uncertainty remains with respect to traveler's response to shoreline protection measures, with research urgently required to explore these fundamental questions. It is clear that Caribbean beach destinations face a two-fold challenge of determining the most effective method to protect their shoreline from projected climate change, while simultaneously adapting in a manner that is acceptable to travelers.

Notes

1. Daniel Scott, Stefan Gössling, and C. Michael Hall. (2012a). "International Tourism and Climate Change." *WIREs Climate Change*, 3. pp. 213–232.

2. Daniel Scott, Bas Amelung, Susanne Becken, John-Paul Ceron, Ghislain Dubois, Stefan Gössling, Paul Peeters, and Murray Simpson. (2008). "Climate Change and Tourism: Responding to Global Challenges." Madrid/Paris/Geneva: UNWTO/UNEP/WMO.

3. Image Source: Michelle Rutty.

4. Daniel Scott, Murray Simpson, and Ryan Sim. (2012b). "The Vulnerability of Caribbean Coastal Tourism to Scenarios of Climate Change Related Sea Level Rise." *Journal of Sustainable Tourism*, 20(6). pp. 883–898.

5. Daniel Scott, Murray Simpson, and Ryan Sim. (2012b). pp. 883–898.

6. Orrin H. Pilkey Jr. and J. Andrew G. Cooper. (2014). *The Last Beach*. North Carolina: Duke University Press.

7. Jacqueline M. Hamilton. (2007). "Coastal Landscape and the Hedonic Price of Accommodation." *Ecological Economics*, 62. pp. 594–602.

8. Jeroen Speybroeck, Dries Bonte, Wouter Courtens, Tom Gheskiere, Patrick Grootaert, Jean-Pierre Maelfait, Mieke Mathys, Sam

Provoost, Koen Sabbe, Eric W.M. Stienen, Vera Van Lancker, Magda Vincx, and Steven Degraer. (2006). "Beach Nourishment: An Ecologically Sound Coastal Defence Alternative? A Review." *Aquatic Conservation: Marine and Freshwater Ecocystems,* 16. pp. 419–435.

9. Mark Stevenson. (2010). "Cancun's Beaches: Vanishing Sand and Wasted Money." *Associated Press.* http://www.spokesman.com/stories /2010/dec/01/cancun-suffers-from-human-climate-impacts/.

10. Mark Stevenson. (2010).

11. Orrin H. Pilkey Jr. and J. Andrew G. Cooper. (2014).

12. Daniel M. Alongi. (2008). "Mangrove Forests: Resilience, Protection from Tsunamis, and Responses to Global Climate Change." *Esturaine, Coastal and Shelf Science,* 76. pp. 1–13.

13. Daniel M. Alongi. (2008). pp. 1–13.

14. Gillian Cambers. (1998). "Planning for Coastline Change: Coastal Development Setback Guidelines in Antigua and Barbuda." Paris: UNESCO.

15. Image Source: Michelle Rutty.

16. Murray C. Simpson, J.F. Clarke, D.J. Scott, M. New, A. Karmalkar, O.J. Day, M. Taylor, S. Gössling, M. Wilson, D. Chadee, N. Fields, H. Stager, R. Waithe, A. Stewart, J. Georges, R. Sim, N. Hutchinson, M. Rutty, L. Matthews, and S. Charles. (2012). *CARIBSAVE Climate Change Risk Atlas.* Barbados: DFID, AusAID, and The Caribsave Partnership: Barbados, West Indies.

17. Kevon Rhiney. (2015). "Geographies of Caribbean Vulnerability in a Changing Climate: Issues and Trends." *Geography Compass,* 9(3). pp. 97–114.

18. Stefan Gössling, Daniel Scott, C. Michael Hall, John-Paul Ceron, and Ghislain Dubois. (2012). "Consumer Behaviour and Demand Response of Tourists to Climate Change." *Annals of Tourism Research,* 39(1). pp. 36–58.

19. Daniel Scott, Stefan Gössling, and C. Michael Hall. (2012a). pp. 213–232.

20. Daniel Scott, Bas Amelung, Susanne Becken, John-Paul Ceron, Ghislain Dubois, Stefan Gössling, Paul Peeters, and Murray Simpson. (2008).

21. Richard Buckley. (2008). "Misperceptions of Climate Change Damage Coastal Tourism: Case Study of Byron Bay, Australia." *Tourism Review International,* 12(1). pp. 71–88.

22. Stefan Gössling, Daniel Scott, C. Michael Hall, John-Paul Ceron, and Ghislain Dubois. (2012). pp. 36–58.

23. Ottmar L. Braun, Martin Lohmann, Olga Maksimovic, Martin Meyer, Anetta Merkovic, Eva Messerschmidt, Annette Riedel, and Marcella Turner. (1999). "Potential Impact of Climate Change Effects on Preferences for Tourism Destinations. A Psychological Pilot Study." *Climate Research,* 11(3). pp. 247–254.

24. Emma G. Coombes and Andy P. Jones. (2010). "Assessing the Impact of Climate Change on Visitor Behaviour and Habitat Use at the Coast: A UK Case Study." *Global Environmental Change,* 20(2). pp. 303–313.

25. Maria C. Uyarra, Isabelle M. Cote, Jennifer A. Gill, Rob R.T. Tinch, David Viner, and Andrew R. Watkinson. (2005). "Island-Specific Preferences of Tourists for Environmental Features: Implications of Climate Change for Tourism-Dependent States." *Environmental Conservation,* 32(1). pp. 11–19.

26. Maria C. Uyarra, Isabelle M. Cote, Jennifer A. Gill, Rob R.T. Tinch, David Viner, and Andrew R. Watkinson. (2005). pp. 11–19.

27. National Oceanic and Atmospheric Administration, Oceanic and Atmospheric Research (NOAA). (2012). *Global Sea Level Rise Scenarios for the United States National Climate Assessment.* U.S. Department of Commerce, NOAA, Climate Program Office.

28. Okmyung Bin, Chris Dumas, Ben Poulter, and John Whitehead. (2007). *Measuring the Impacts of Climate Change on North Carolina Coastal Resources.* Washington: National Commission on Energy Policy.

29. Christine N. Buzinde, David Manuel-Navarrete, Eunice E. Yoo, and Duarte Morais. (2010). "Tourists' Perceptions in a Climate of Change. Eroding destinations." *Annals of Tourism Research,* 37(2). pp. 333–354.

30. M.D. Kudale, A.V. Mahalingaiah, and B.R. Tayade. (2014). "Use of Sand-Filled Geotextile Tubes for Sustainable Coastal Protection – Case Studies in Indian Scenario." *Indian Journal of Marine Sciences*, 43(7). pp. 1–7.

31. Image Source: Geofrabrics Australasia.

32. Jacqueline M. Hamilton. (2007). pp. 594–602.

33. Jacqueline M. Hamilton. (2007). pp. 594–602.

34. Daniel Scott, Murray Simpson, and Ryan Sim. (2012b). pp. 883–898.

35. Christine N. Buzinde, David Manuel-Navarrete, Eunice E. Yoo, and Duarte Morais. (2010). pp. 333–354.

Case Study 2.3

Building Coastal Destination Resilience in the Dominican Republic

by Paul Guggenheim

The Dominican Republic (DR) is heavily dependent on coastal tourism, making it highly susceptible to risks associated with climate change, including increases in ocean temperatures, SLR, and annual decline in precipitation. With much of the country's economic interests vested in the health of its coastline, it should be a wake-up call to have been listed as the world's eighth most vulnerable country to climate change in the Global Climate Risk Index 2014.[1] For an island nation like the Dominican Republic, the environmental effects of climate change can significantly degrade the biodiversity, health, and environmental productivity of coastal ecosystems, including coral reefs, mangroves, and sea grass beds. Climate change also threatens the productivity and stability of the Dominican economy and workforce, which is closely tied to the country's tourism industry.

Counterpart International, a U.S.-based nonprofit development organization, has worked in the Dominican Republic since 2004 in partnership with local organizations and communities to combat climate change threats. This has been done through local capacity building and implementing strategies to help strengthen communities' ability to ensure sustainable livelihoods that depend upon healthy ecosystems. By taking a holistic and integrated approach to coastal ecosystems, the Dominican Republic can ensure that its most valued resources required for international tourism and economic growth are sustained and ensured for future generations.

To be economically viable, socially beneficial, and environmentally sustainable, coastal tourism must build and operate based on the realities and projected impacts of climate change. The government's National Development Strategy of the Dominican Republic 2010 to 2030 identifies "sustainable environmental management and adequate adaptation to climate change" as one of the government's four strategic areas. Some national efforts have been positive and visionary, including those of the DR Climate Council established in 2008, with "the objective of coordinating and joining efforts from the various institutions that make up the country's development, to combat the global problem of climate change."[2] In addition, the Ministry of Environment has taken steps for Reducing Emissions from Deforestation and Forest Degradation Plus (REDD+) by establishing a course to create a financial value for the carbon stored in forests. The *plus* represents REDD elements added in 2010, which include the enhancement of forest carbon stocks. However, while the Dominican Republic has a number of plans, policies, and laws that support REDD+ activities, it has no overarching national strategy in practice.

Further, while the DR is the first country in the Caribbean to develop a National Climate Compatible Development Plan (CCDP),[3] in practice the government's tourism strategy is not sufficiently protecting coastal resources or addressing the realities of climate change. And in some instances government policies and practices are at odds with its stated commitment to combat climate change. In recent years, for instance, the Dominican Republic has sought to position itself as a leading destination for *sun-and-sand tourism* through the rapid growth of all-inclusive coastal resorts. In 2012, President Danilo Medina set a national tourism target to double international arrivals from 5 to 10 million annually over the course of 10 years—and this goal is expected to be attainable, according to the DR Central Bank.[4] Through the introduction of Law 195-13 and modification of Article 6 of Law 158-01, the government is offering incentives for tourism developers, including no taxes on new buildings and renovations for 10 to 15 years.[5]

These national tourism targets based on growth in arrival numbers are straining the very resources that visitors come to the DR to enjoy. As a counter balance, the government, with international support has launched a program to engage the tourism sector in biodiversity protection[6] and to enable the Ministries of Tourism and Environment and Natural Resources to assess and propose integration of biodiversity goals[7] into the National Tourism Strategy. However, the government has not established or enforced environmental sustainability action plans for addressing climate change.

While government-endorsed large-scale coastal tourism infrastructure and marketing efforts continue, Counterpart International believes an important opportunity exists to cultivate and expand local, ecological, community tourism in order to help manage and protect the country's coastal natural resources. Around the country, Counterpart International and its partners have identified numerous opportunities to integrate and develop community participation that builds on local culture and identity. Active community participation is key for the conservation of natural resources and protection of local livelihoods, as well as for the successful adoption of strategies to address climate change.

In line with the National Development Strategy's stated priorities to address climate change, Counterpart is focusing on climate change resilience and educational activities to help create more sustainable ways for communities to generate revenue through tourism-related activities while being mindful of their environment. To facilitate this effort, Counterpart established the *Coastal Community Resilience Framework* for the Dominican Republic[8] to guide its work with partner communities, organizations, and the public and private sectors.

Over the past 10 years Counterpart has worked with communities and local and international organizations[9] to develop successful programs related to *blue carbon*[i], coral gardens, *ridge to reef*,[ii] sustainable tourism, and youth development training programs. Counterpart's goal is to increase the role of coastal communities in maintaining sustainable climate-resilient ecosystem services, while strengthening opportunities in the tourism industry. The three objectives of the Framework are to:

- Enable and strengthen the multisector national level dialogue to improve policies that support resilience;
- Enhance the capacity of local institutions to formulate, advocate for, and implement improved coastal climate resilience strategies and programs; and
- Increase youth opportunities for coastal conservation education and engagement.

---

[i] Blue carbon is a term used to describe the carbon captured by the world's ocean and coastal ecosystems.

[ii] Ridge to Reef is an integrated approach to land, water, forest, biodiversity, and coastal resource management that contributes to poverty reduction, sustainable livelihoods, and climate resilience

The following are three examples of Counterpart projects that seek to put the *Coastal Community Resilience Framework* into practice.

Mangrove Restoration and Increased Recreation Potential

In recent decades, the DR lost more than 50 percent of its mangroves, primarily due to tourism, shrimp farming, and other types of coastal development. In 2014, Counterpart, in an effort to promote linkages between sound science and public policy, published a blue carbon study focused on mangroves in the Montecristi National Park.[10] The study revealed extraordinarily high levels of carbon stocks stored in the mangrove sites tested, and comparatively low stocks stored in nearby lands composed of abandoned shrimp ponds, which had formerly been mangroves. The government's Climate Council recognized that these findings demonstrate the potential of healthy mangroves for carbon mitigation and increased climate resilience. The Council asked Counterpart to develop a Nationally Appropriate Mitigation Action (NAMA), a voluntary national-level project focused on blue carbon that conforms to the United Nations Framework Convention on Climate Change (UNFCCC). Counterpart's program to expand mangrove conservation throughout the DR is designed to both mitigate climate change by increasing the capture of greenhouse gases in the atmosphere and to enhance coastal communities' climate resilience through eco-services provided by mangrove systems. Based on this concept, in June 2015, the DR government registered the first ever Blue Carbon NAMA in the UNFCCC's NAMA Registry, a database for NAMA projects proposed around the world.[11]

The NAMA proposes a six-point plan to build the capacity of the DR to quantify its blue carbon stocks and establish a sound Monitoring, Reporting, and Verification (MRV) system. Monitoring stations are to double as education centers around the country. Reforestation of mangroves also benefits local communities through increased tourism activities such as kayaking and bird watching in Samaná Bay, Montecristi, and Puerto Plata. Key to the strategy is identifying and applying mechanisms whereby local communities can benefit economically.

Image 2.3.1 Oysters on mangroves in Manzanillo, Montecristi[12]

Currently in the DR, tourism around mangrove ecosystems occurs on a small scale, with visitors experiencing these magnificent ecosystems through guided boat tours in Estero Balsa National Park on the north coast and los Haiteses in Samaná Bay. The planned NAMA will help to expand these recreational activities, thus increasing economic opportunities for local communities. In Puerto Plata, where a newly restored cruise port is dramatically increasing tourism arrivals, Counterpart and its partners are working with the community of Punta Rusia to strengthen local tourism attractions and activities so that coastal residents can benefit from the expanding tourism. Community projects include restoring a small central park, providing a public shower, creating murals with environmental messages, zoning the beaches for swimming, recreation, artisanal fishing, promoting snorkeling in an offshore underwater coral nursery, and improving safety through access to lifesaving vests, reliable boats, and first aid supplies. The project has also organized a community business committee to oversee development of a business plan for community-based tourism.

With heightened awareness of mangroves' climate mitigation benefits, mangrove restoration is becoming a greater tourism attraction. In addition, mangroves also serve as buffers to storm swells, filters for contamination, and habitat for improved biodiversity.

Image 2.3.2 Counterpart and local partners AgroFontera surveying rice farms, Montecristi[13]

Farmers and Fishers Collaborate on Ecosystem Protection

In the northwest corner of the country, bordering Haiti, Montecristi province is home to multiple ecosystems, including some of the healthiest, near-shore coral reefs, significant mangrove systems, and dry coastal forests. It is also a region with significant agriculture and ranching, including rice, bananas, and cattle.

More than one-third of DR's rice comes from this region, with approximately 15,000 hectares of rice production taking place in a complex of canals. Unfortunately, these canals drain chemical-laced wastewater from rice farming directly into the Estero Balsa mangrove system, which is one of five protected areas in Montecristi. Along the eastern side bordering Puerto Plata, there is a burgeoning tourism industry with potential for community participation.

Since 2010 Counterpart has been helping rice growers to reduce the use of pesticides and fertilizers[iii] and improve their labor techniques with

---

[iii] With support from the John D. and Catherine T. MacArthur Foundation, in collaboration with local partner AgroFrontera and the Inter-American Development Bank.

the aim of reducing nutrient loads into the canals, lowering costs of production, and maximizing yields. Today, conditions are improving in the mangroves, adjacent estuarial zones, and nearby coral reefs, all-important areas for the community-based tourism and fisheries' economies.

Counterpart also works with fisher communities to establish best practices for achieving a balance between ecosystem protection and improved livelihoods. Counterpart helps local fishers to better understand and observe seasonal rules, fish sizes, net sizes, and regulations for fishing equipment, as well as types of fish that should and should not be caught. For example, at present, parrotfish and related species that feed around coral reefs are not protected. Yet these colorful species are extremely important for both tourism and coral reef health. Parrotfish feed on coral algae, cleaning and pruning the reef, and making coral sand bits that pass out of their digestive system. A single parrotfish can produce up to several hundred pounds of white sand in one year. However, because many other traditionally consumed fish populations have been depleted, the parrotfish is now over-fished. According to one study, "In the case of the coral-reef fishery of Buen Hombre, parrotfish play a critical role in ecosystem functioning and they comprise half of the fishermen's catch."[14] Counterpart has helped organize hundreds of fishers in six communities, stretching along 80 miles of coastline in Montecristi National Park. With more organization and awareness of their reliance on local natural resources, these fishers have become stewards of the coastline. As a result, at least one group of fishers regularly reports to the authorities any unregulated behavior or illegal fishing practices. Fishers report that before they participated in the Counterpart program, they had never worked together to protect their resources.

Youth Opportunities for Learning and Conservation

Counterpart has partnered with eight private, bilingual schools in Santo Domingo, the country's capital, to introduce collaborative opportunities for learning about marine biology and to participate in conservation activities through hands-on coastal biomonitoring. Middle and upper school teachers are being trained to empower their students to look beyond the classroom and to establish learning communities to better understand the risks of climate change and strengthen coastal community resilience.

By recording data through scientific protocols, the students are collecting valuable information to help grade and chart over time the health of their coastal research sites.

These participating schools have now formed an association, the Dominican Environmental Education Program (DEEP), the country's first collaboration among schools to address climate change. A group of Santo Domingo university students trained in marine biology and conservation serve as peer mentors. A collection of national and international organizations specializing in coastal marine conservation have also formed a learning community to support these schools with technical assistance and hands-on learning experiences. Together, with this team, Counterpart is building a cadre of youth leaders to serve as a source for sound scientific data and technical analysis and to help community-based organizations take resilience actions at the local, regional, and national levels.

Conclusions

Community participation is an essential element for achieving success in both sustainable tourism projects and climate change resilience. While national and international investment is essential for the development of effective tourism, partnerships at the local level are critical to achieving long-term sustainability. Approaches should build on experiences that respect local history and culture and incorporate innovation into planning. These include strategic and action planning for community resilience, peer-to-peer learning, and a youth leadership training through inquiry-based teaching methodology. The partnerships Counterpart has forged in the DR have proven that protecting natural resources within a country dependent on coastal and marine tourism can both help to protect the resource base essential for tourism and ensure local residents have improved livelihoods and greater protection against the impacts of climate change.

Notes

1. Sönke Kreft and David Eckstein. (2014). "Table 1: The Long-Term Climate Risk Index (CRI): Results (annual averages) in Specific Indicators in the 10 Countries Most Affected from 1993 to

2012," *Global Climate Risk Index.* https://germanwatch.org/en /download/8551.pdf.

2. The National Council for Climate Change and Clean Development Mechanism (CNCCMDL). (2013). http://translate.google.com /translate?hl=en&sl=es&tl=en&u=http%3A%2F%2Fccclimatico .wordpress.com%2.

3. The REDD Desk. (2016). *REDD in Dominican Republic.* http:// theredddesk.org/countries/dominican-republic.

4. Amilcar Nivar. (2015). "El Banco Central Destaca Meta de 10 Millones de Turistas es Alcanzable en RD." *Diario Libre.* http:// www.diariolibre.com/economia/economia-personal/el-banco -central-destaca-meta-de-10-millones-de-turistas-es-alcanzable-en -rd-AJDL983641.

5. Enrique E. De Marchena Kaluche LLB. (2014). "Executive Summary Law 195-13, Enacted 13 December 2013, Amending Law 158-01, Dated 9 October 2001, on Promoting Tourism Development." *DMK Lawyers.* http://www.dmklawyers.com/EN /publications/266-executive-summary-law-195-13-enacted-13 -december-2013-amending-law-158-01-dated-9-october-2001-on -promoting-tourism-development.html.

6. Agencia EFE. (November 6, 2015). "Realizan Seminario sobre Bioversidad y Turismo en RD." *Amo Dominicano.* http://www .amodominicana.com/2015/11/06/realizan-seminario-sobre -biodiversidad-y-turismo-en-rd/.

7. UNDP. (February 3, 2016). "Medio Ambiente, MITUR y PNUD Impulsan Conservacion de la Bioversidad Costera para Garantizar el Desarollo Turistico y la Sostenibilidad." UNDP in Dominican Republic. http://www.do.undp.org/content/dominican_republic/es /home/presscenter/articles/2016/02/03/medio-ambiente-mitur -y-pnud-impulsan-conservaci-n-de-la-biodiversidad-costera-para -garantizar-el-desarrollo-tur-stico-y-la-sostenibilidad.html

8. Counterpart International. (2016). "Coastal Community Resilience Program (Dominican Republic)." http://www.counterpart.org/coastal -community-resilience-program/

9. Puntacana Ecological Foundation (PCEF), AgroFrontera, CIBIMA, CEBSE, the National Council on Climate Change and the Clean

Development Mechanism (CNCCMDL), the University of Miami, and Oregon State University.

10. J. Boone Kaufman, Chris Heider, Jennifer Norfolk, and Frederick Payton. (2014). "Carbon Stocks from Intact Mangroves and Carbon Emissions Arising from their Conversion in the Dominican Republic." *Ecological Applications,* 24(3). pp. 518–527.

11. UNFCCC. (2015). "Blue Carbon NAMA: Conserve and Restore Mangroves in the Dominican Republic." *NAMA Profiles.* https:// unfccc.int/files/cooperation_support/nama/application/pdf /dr_blue_carbon_nama_final.pdf. UNFCCC. (2015). "NS-189- Blue Carbon NAMA: Conserve and Restore Mangroves in the Dominican Republic," *Public NAMAs.* http://www4.unfccc.int/sites /nama/_layouts/un/fccc/nama/NamaSeekingSupportForPreparation .aspx?ID=115&viewOnly=1.

12. Image Source: Paul Guggenheim.

13. Image Source: Paul Guggenheim.

14. Tyler Pavlowich and Gillian O. Britton. (2013). "Using Details of Coral-reef Fishers' Harvest, Including Taxonomic and Size-structure, to Support Ecosystem-based Fisheries Management in Montecristi National Park, Dominican Republic." *Proceedings of the 66th Gulf and Caribbean Fisheries Institute.* pp.96–99.

CHAPTER 3

Siting, Architecture, Design, and Construction

Overview—Adapting to the *New Normal* from Siting through Construction

Denaye Hinds and Esteban Biondi

For resort developments throughout the Caribbean, shorelines and beaches have always been considered the prime locations. In siting a resort, most developers have traditionally looked for the same thing: an oceanfront setting within earshot of the waves, easy beach access, and beautiful views of the sea. While the Caribbean boasts no shortage of coastal real estate, site selection and development must carefully follow specific guidelines. In this era of climate change, coastal sites are particularly vulnerable. Siting is extremely important, but it's only the first step: the architectural, design, and construction phases of a tourism project also must incorporate the latest in sustainable best practices in order to assess vulnerabilities and minimize risk. Although the fundamental tools of sustainable coastal development are not yet widely used in the Caribbean to address the present hurricane risk, we now have to add consideration for increased vulnerabilities due to climate change.

As we come to better understand how climate change is affecting what has been assumed to be the Caribbean norm of "stepping out of your room and onto the sandy beach," we need to redefine, diversify, and innovate the design and construction of tourism facilities and attractions.

In doing so, new strategies that incorporate adaptive capacities and resilience while maintaining function, form, and aesthetic are emerging. The new way of master planning and building requires that present risks and climate change projections are incorporated into the siting, architecture, design, and construction so that resorts can weather the impacts of more frequent and/or intense storms, sea level rise, and other phenomena linked to climate change.

Kevin Trenberth, a senior scientist at the National Center for Atmospheric Research, reminds us that climate change is manmade: "Global warming is contributing to an increased incidence of extreme weather because the environment in which all storms form has changed from human activities."[1] Human activities such as irresponsible waste management, burning of fossil fuels for electricity generation, and carbon-intensive construction and materials are contributors to climate change. Across the region we are already experiencing the effects: from droughts and extended dry seasons, to coral reef, sea grass, and mangrove loss; storm surge, flooding, and mudslides; and new pests and diseases that ultimately threaten our built, human, and natural environments.

A range of factors, including sourcing and consumption of natural resources and waste management, also need to be incorporated into the development and operations of tourism projects. However, while many best practices are aimed at addressing the root causes of climate change, additional measures are needed to mitigate the changes that are already inevitable.

Public policies to encourage and support smart planning, sustainable design, and responsible construction are required to help ensure that tourism business will successfully adapt to the challenges we face in the wake of climate variance and sea level rise. Private developers who thoroughly evaluate projects with an emphasis on return on investments can also justify adopting sustainable and resilient design.

The following sections look at sustainability and climate resilient needs and adaptive strategies for the siting, architecture, design, and construction of coastal and island resorts. While these four steps are interconnected and often overlapping, they also each require specialized skills, specific considerations, and tailored solutions.

Siting: Adapting to the *New Normal*

Given the realities of the *new normal* in the Caribbean, increased setback distances and alternative inland locations may afford more economical and environmentally sustainable alternatives (Chapter 2 Overview Essay). Hotels and other tourism infrastructure and attractions built inland not only reduce the dangers facing ocean-front structures, but can also can offer spectacular coastal and ocean vistas, lush natural surroundings, and a range of activities more suitable to interior island locations—such as hiking, biking, and organic farming, to name a few (Case Study 3.2). In cases where significant setbacks or inland siting may not be possible or suitable, adaptive reuse of existing coastal tourism structures and a growing number of "green" technologies for design and construction may help to preserve coastal attributes and resources (Case Study 3.3).

Siting and location, including policies that provide for appropriate setbacks, zoning, and land use, have significant effects on a property's insurability, performance, durability, and resilience, both in the short and long terms. To understand and accomplish appropriate siting, islands must first understand and map their tourism capacity and resources. Appropriate tourism siting and destination management creates the framework for sustainable tourism development, which can reduce the likelihood of adverse weather-related effects. Caribbean countries need to create and/or update their land use plans for tourism development. For instance, the Bermuda National Tourism Plan of 2012 proposed creating five new distinct *tourism hubs* offering distinct cultural and natural tourism attractions.[2]

Coastal setbacks are put in place to protect structures and shorelines from the effects of storms and erosion. A CARIBSAVE study developed an equation for setback of buildings on coasts and shorelines, accounting for the contribution of different effects: acute erosion, chronic erosion, sea level rise, and safety factors. The equation proposed for determining setback is:

Setback Distance $= (A + B + C) \times D$, with:

- **A** is the setback distance needed to account for acute erosion from a major storm event;
- **B** is the additional setback distance needed to account for long-term processes that create conditions for chronic erosion;

- **C** is the added distance needed to account for sea level rise impacts; and
- **D** is a safety factor that increases as uncertainty increases or to account for ecological planning or social considerations.[3]

Acute erosion and wave impacts due to extreme events, long-term erosion processes, and sea level rise can be evaluated quantitatively using specialized coastal engineering tools. Historical data for extreme event analysis and to evaluate long-term trends can be obtained from international sources and models, so lack of local records in the Caribbean is no longer a major problem for most engineering analyses. FEMA's *Coastal Construction Manual*[4] and the determination of flood zones following methodologies used in the United States are available as a complementary analytical method to recommend horizontal and vertical setbacks. Coupled with appropriate zoning to encourage smart planning and reduce pressure on infrastructure, these serve as a primary strategy for sustainable siting.

Many Caribbean countries have set legal setbacks from the high water mark (Chapter 2 Overview Essay) and these regulations, combined with natural buffers contribute to more responsible coastal development. However, legal setbacks are typically defined in general (not technical) terms and may not be enough or may be more conservative than is needed. When technical studies are not publicly available, site-specific engineering studies undertaken by developers may provide more accurate recommendations for setbacks and structural design. The use of engineering analysis also allows for testing more resilient and innovative designs. For example, in the wake of hurricane damage to its mangroves, the Ritz Carlton Grand Cayman conceived a redevelopment master plan that included restoration of mangroves and implementation of other environmentally sensitive storm protection measures (Case Study 3.1).

Open space protection and smart use of land for the public good are also imperative in the Caribbean, given the limited land available for development. Public policies must also balance siting and planning of tourism resorts and attractions with an island's residential needs. For instance, as the chapter on golf courses elaborates (Vol. 2, Chapter 2 Overview Essay), given the amount of land needed to build a course, the cost and environmental impacts of construction and maintenance, and the declining

Image 3.0.1 Rendering of Ritz Carlton Grand Cayman[5]

interest in golf playing in the United States, careful consideration needs to be given to whether building more golf courses in the Caribbean is a wise economic—as well as social and environmental—investment.

Integrated landscape and green spaces also play significant roles in smart planning. Creation of green spaces by the shoreline can help buffer against storms while also providing seamless and natural setbacks of buildings. Planting drought tolerant and native species in those spaces can reduce water use.

In addition to new buildings on new sites, redevelopment on existing sites, building repurposing, and multi-use design contribute to smart planning and design strategies (Case Study 3.3). Encouraging redevelopment of existing sites, such as brownfields,[i] and cleaning up and reinvesting in these properties helps to protect the environment, reduces blight, and takes development pressures off green spaces and working landscapes, according to the U.S. Environmental Protection Agency (EPA).[6] The economic recession that began in 2008 had a major impact on the Caribbean's tourism sector, causing business decline, failed projects, and stalled construction. Buildings once occupied or partially constructed offer opportunities for repurposing. New innovations such as pop-up restaurants and mobile shops provide new models that can reduce coastal development.

---

[i] A brownfield is a site to be used for housing or business that had been previously used for industry and may be contaminated or need extensive clearing.

Architecture: Redesigning for Sustainability and Climate Change

Former U.S. Vice President Al Gore's Climate Reality Project Training[7] challenges the architecture profession to play a much bigger role in implementing design-based sustainable strategies to address climate change. Historically, designers have relied on past data regarding storms, weather events, and potential architectural failures. Instead, through simulation and modeling for anticipated future extreme and uncertain weather conditions—hurricanes, drought, tsunamis, earthquakes, severe flooding, landslides—architects can design to avoid catastrophic or irreversible failures. For example, by simulating the impacts of a 130 mph hurricane onto their plans, architects can gain knowledge and address building weaknesses, stressors, and potential failures prior to design completion. They are able to incorporate resilient design strategies such as hurricane rated doors; triple-glazed, dual low-e windows; and storm-resistant louvers.

In addition, there is growing recognition that, as the Resilient Design Institute puts it, "Simple, passive and flexible systems are more resilient"[8] and have the ability to adapt to the changing conditions in both the short and long term. Resilient design includes passive survivability systems such as natural ventilation, cooling through use of cross-trade winds, solar panels to supplement natural daylighting, and passive heating based on sun patterns. For water conservation, resilient design includes rainwater harvesting and gravity fed systems in the event of power failure. The resilience of renewable energy—wind and solar—can be increased with efficient battery-storage at high elevations. Durable design and materials include deep roof overhangs to protect buildings from extreme wind and rains, rot-resistant and fast-drying materials, tread rails and grid flooring to reduce moisture and improve durability, curved roof designs to reduce wind damage, and *kit of part*[ii] doors and materials in which a damaged piece may be replaced rather than the entire door.

Highly technical coastal protection, storm water management, and resilient structural design should be functionally and aesthetically engineered into the architectural elements of resorts. Embedding natural systems and re-creating environmental features as part of the design are

---

[ii] *Kit of part* refers to prefabricated materials.

also best practices that enhance the value of resort projects, often at a cost reduction, which justifies implementation by developers.

A growing number of specific newer architectural and design techniques (applicable to coastal developments) that help to promote sustainability and address climate change illustrate these concepts:

- **Bioswales** are "storm water runoff conveyance systems that provide an alternative to storm sewers. They can absorb low flows or carry runoff from heavy rains to storm sewer inlets or directly to surface waters. Bioswales improve water quality by infiltrating the first flush of storm water runoff"[9] and providing filtering. They should be part of a comprehensive storm water management system that is designed for both flood control and water quality objectives, and can be *hidden* as part of the landscape design.
- **Rain gardens** are "landscaped to collect, store, and absorb storm water runoff in its loose underlying soil. Rain gardens are strategically placed to intercept storm water runoff and hold it until it can be fully absorbed into the ground." [10]
- **Green or Living walls** incorporate vegetation in their structure or on their surface, and do not require the plants to be rooted in substrate at the base of the wall.[11]

Image 3.0.2 Rain Garden at Oregon Convention Center[12]

- **Roof garden or Green roofs** are gardens that are built on existing roofs and involve high-quality waterproofing and root repellant systems, drainage systems, filter cloth, lightweight growing medium, and plants. Green roofs last longer than conventional roofs, reduce energy costs with natural insulation, create peaceful retreats for people and animals, and absorb storm water, potentially lessening the need for complex and expensive drainage systems.[13]
- **Interlocking concrete pavers** are hand-sized, rectangular or dentated units placed in an interlocking pattern and compacted into a thin bedding layer. The paving units and bedding create a durable paving surface for pedestrians and vehicles[14] with more permeability than regular pavers.

Tourism and its built environment have the ability not only to show-case resilient architecture and design, but also to educate, inspire, engage, and influence other sectors. Take, for instance, a beachfront resort and conference center in South Florida showcased by the Urban Land Institute (ULI) publication, *Returns on Resilience: The Business Case*.[15] According to ULI, the resort (unnamed by the publication) is being redeveloped to show "how investments that address climate change risks can also benefit the bottom line with more effective marketing, better financing terms, and lower insurance premiums and energy bills." Its resilience features include relocating the electrical infrastructure above the known storm surge level; installing hurricane-resistant windows and doors; an on-site backup power system with generators and diesel fuel storage tank; and on-site water desalination wells and water storage tank. These climate-wise changes have boosted the resort's insurable value by 50 percent; saved $685,000 a year on insurance, energy, and water; and created a more competitive conference business that can guarantee clients that conferences will not be interrupted or cancelled because of intense hurricanes and tropical storm surges.

Design: Resilience and Science-Based Engineering Analysis

Best practices for the design of coastal destinations include science -based quantitative analysis of coastal risks, qualitative assessment of uncertainties, and an approach that incorporates resilience elements and environmental features to the design, which add value to the project. Most coastal developments in the Caribbean, and especially coastal resort projects, have not been properly designed to withstand hurricane conditions such as storm surges and waves. The first approach to climate change adaptation is to ensure that design guidelines for present hurricane risk conditions are met. Once this first tier analysis is undertaken, the projected modifications required to address climate change can be incorporated.

The best practice for coastal construction is to find design solutions that contain structural resilience and add economic value to the project. According to ULI, resilience is "the ability to prepare and plan for, absorb, recover from, and more successfully adapt to adverse events." Coastal structures built with resilience facilitate recovery after an extreme event, permit for incremental damage as opposed to sudden collapse if the design conditions are exceeded, and allow for additional enhancements when repaired. Resilient design approaches allow for recovery after storms to *bounce forward*, or easily incorporate further improvements during repairs, as opposed to *only bounce back* to prestorm conditions. Other available resilience strategies, such as the ones compiled by ULI,[16] are still not followed in most Caribbean projects.

FEMA's *Coastal Construction Manual* has established guidelines based on calculating storm conditions with an average probability of occurrence once every 100 years (or 1 percent probability for any given year). Construction criteria are then recommended for the so-called *100-year storm*. The *base flood elevation*, which is the highest predicted water elevation including wave effects, is used as a reference design parameter. The guidelines recommend that utilities and living spaces should be above the base flood elevation (plus a freeboard for additional safety) and that buildings be designed to allow the ocean energy to pass unobstructed without damage to structural supports. Sea level rise impacts can be considered by following the same methodology but using increased sea level scenarios. This information allows coastal engineers to provide recommendations for siting of coastal development based on site-specific quantitative analysis.

In the United States, the FEMA Flood Insurance Program requires that coastal properties follow specific construction guidelines, and FEMA provides the data based on flood maps. In the Caribbean, most island states have not developed that information, and many government agencies only have basic requirements based on past experiences, such as legal setbacks or road elevations that were not flooded in past storms. However, scientific-based parameters can be calculated using FEMA's guidelines. While real estate developers in the Caribbean may have to invest in specific studies when the information is not available from the government, it is arguably beneficial because it permits better design and sometimes lowers construction costs. This may reduce insurance premiums, and can be used to show investors and lenders that the best practices and best available technical tools were used for design.

Construction: Reducing GHG Emissions and Increasing Resilience

There's good news here: rapid advances are being made in construction methods and techniques that are reducing GHG emissions. Innovative solutions such as 3D printing of materials and prefabricated buildings are changing the construction landscape, shortening the construction time, and reducing the energy required to build. Off-site, prefabricated construction techniques are gaining popularity. These may offer more resilience and strength and also reduce waste and pollution because construction takes place within a controlled environment as opposed to on-site.

Traditional construction is being replaced with insulated concrete forms (ICFs) that integrate 100 percent recycled materials, reduce waste and carbon emissions, and use less machinery, thereby reducing GHG emissions while not compromising building strength and durability. For example, one ICF system, Nudura®,[17] provides disaster resilience performance in withstanding impacts from fire and high winds while improving building energy performance. The system incorporates steel-reinforced concrete, layered between two continuous panels of EPS (expanded polystyrene) foam. This isolates the concrete and creates an airtight structure, provides long-term energy efficiency, and improves indoor air quality.

There are also a number of certification programs developed for commercial buildings that are beginning to be used in the design, construction, and operation of sustainable coastal tourism resorts and hotels. They include methods and techniques for sustainable site selection, construction processes, material selection, energy efficiency, water preservation, and resilience. These programs include:

- **LEED (Leadership in Energy and Environmental Design)** is a certification system of the U.S. Green Building Council. It verifies a building's or neighborhood's *green features*,[1] which are assessed according to the location of the site, water, and energy efficiency and the use of materials and resources. The criteria depend on the category to which the assessed site belongs: Building Design and Construction, Interior Design and Construction, Building Operations and Management, Neighborhood Development, and Homes.[18] There are a handful of LEED-certified resorts and hotels in the Caribbean, including Bucuti & Tara Beach Resorts in Aruba (Case Study 4.2).
- **The Living Building Challenge (LBC)** is a certification program of the Living Future Institute. Any kind of building, be it new or existing, can be certified according to seven performance categories, the so-called *petals*: Place, Water, Energy, Health and Happiness, Materials, Equity, and Beauty.[19] So far there is only one registered LBC building in the Caribbean, a Marine Research and Education Center in Puerto Rico.[20]
- **WELL Building Standard** is a certification system administered by the International WELL Building Institute (IWBI). It focuses on features of the built environment that have an impact on human health and well-being by looking at seven factors: air, water, nourishment, light, fitness, comfort, and mind.[21] In the Caribbean there are at present seven WELL Building Standard projects in Barbados, one in Belize, and one in Haiti.[22]
- **The Sustainable Sites Initiative (SITES)** is a certification system that can be applied to open spaces without buildings, streetscapes, and plazas, as well as to all kinds of buildings larger than 2,000 square feet. The assessment of a site includes its context; the management of water, soil, and vegetation; use of materials; the well-being and health of the local population; and the construction, operation, and maintenance of buildings. The rating system also includes education and performance monitoring and innovative or exemplary performance.[23] The program has the ability to address increasingly urgent global concerns such as loss of biodiversity, resource depletion, and climate change.[24] To date, there are no SITES-certified buildings in the Caribbean.

Programs such as these, together with the sustainable tourism certification programs already in use in the Caribbean (Chapter 4 Overview
Essay), offer concrete tools for ensuring sustainable design, construction,
and operations of coastal hotels and other infrastructure and for reducing
the impacts of climate change.

Conclusion

The urgent call to action to include climate change resilience within siting,
architecture, design, and construction is evident. We can no longer afford
to blindly develop without taking the consequence into consideration.
The encouraging news is that—despite all the mistakes of the past and
present—multiple initiatives from every corner of the hospitality development industry are underway. The professional contributions of architects, planners, and engineers continue to evolve with best practices, and
can be major drivers of change by providing innovative practical solutions
and offering technical advice to developers and governments. Professional
institutions and organizations are already documenting that smart coastal
development is both economically sound and the most effective business
decision, for both public and private entities. Resilient and sustainable
design is growing in acceptance by some pioneering private developers
and should become mainstream as investors and insurance companies
recognize the inherent economic value of these approaches. Regulatory
agencies and communities are incorporating frameworks that account for
climate change, which both raise the bar and level the field for the real
estate business. These actions can converge into effective results.

Notes

1. Al Neuharth. (2011). "Can We Do Anything about Vicious
   Bad Weather?" *USA Today*. http://usatoday30.usatoday.com/news
   /opinion/forum/2011-06-03-Were-weatherbeaten-but-are-we
   -weatherwise_n.htm.
2. Bermuda Tourism Authority, T&L Tourism Leisure and Sports,
   Europraxis and OBM International (OBMI). (June 11, 2012).
   Bermuda National Tourism Master Plan. Town Hall Presentation.

http://www.gotobermuda.com/uploadedFiles/Bermuda_Tourism_Authority/Pages/Bermuda-National-Tourism-Master-Plan.pdf.

3. Murray C. Simpson, Colleen Mercer Clarke, John D. Clarke, Daniel Scott, and Alexander Clarke. (2012). *Coastal Setbacks in Latin America and the Caribbean: Final Report.* A study of emerging issues and trends that inform guidelines for coastal planning and development. InterAmerican Development Bank.

4. FEMA. (2011). *Coastal Construction Manual: Principles and Practices of Planning, Siting, Designing, Constructing, and Maintaining Residential Buildings in Coastal Areas.* 4th Edition. p.55. http://www.fema.gov/rebuild/mat/fema55.shtm.

5. Image Source: Dan Cross.

6. EPA. (October 2015). "Enhancing Communities with Green Infrastructure." https://www.epa.gov/smartgrowth/about-smart-growth.

7. The Climate Reality Project—Climate Reality Leadership Corps, Florida. (2015). https://www.climaterealityproject.org/.

8. Resilient Design Institute (RDI). http://www.resilientdesign.org/resilient-design-strategies/.

9. Natural Resources Conservation Service. (2005). "Bioswales." http://www.nrcs.usda.gov/Internet/FSE_DOCUMENTS/nrcs144p2_029251.pdf.

10. District of Columbia Department of Energy and Environment. "RiverSmart Homes: Rain Gardens." http://doee.dc.gov/service/riversmart-homes-rain-gardens.

11. R.A. Francis. & J. Lorimer. (2011). "Urban Reconciliation Ecology: The Potential of Living Roofs and Walls." *Journal of Environmental Management,* 92. pp. 1429-1437.

12. Image Source: Nancy Erz/Travel Portland.

13. Green Roofs for Healthy Cities. "About Green Roofs." http://www.greenroofs.org/index.php/about/aboutgreenroofs; Sarah Dowdey. (July 11, 2007). "What is a Green Roof?" http://science.howstuffworks.com/environmental/green-science/green-rooftop.htm.

14. Interlocking Concrete Paving Institute (ICPI). "Pavement Types." https://www.icpi.org/paving-systems.

15. Urban Land Institute (2015). *Returns on Resilience: The Business Case.* ULI Center for Sustainability. Washington, D.C.: Urban

Land Institute. pp. 27-29. http://uli.org/wp-content/uploads/ULI
-Documents/Returns-on-Resilience-The-Business-Case.pdf.

16. Urban Land Institute. (April 2015). *A Guide to Assessing Climate
Change Risk.* Washington, D.C.: Urban Land Institute. http://
uli.org/wp-content/uploads/ULI-Documents/ULI-A-Guide-for
-Assessesing-Climate-Change-Risk-final.pdf.

17. Nadura. http://www.nudura.com/.

18. U.S. Green Building Council. "This is LEED." http://leed.usgbc.org
/leed.html; U.S. Green Building Council (2016). "Checklist: LEED
v4 for Building Design and Construction." http://www.usgbc.org
/resources/leed-v4-building-design-and-construction-checklist; U.S.
Green Building Council. "LEED." http://www.usgbc.org/leed.

19. International Living Future Institute. "Living Building Challenge
3.0." http://living-future.org/lbc/about.

20. International Living Future Institute. "Registered Living Building
Challenge Projects." http://living-future.org/projectmap.

21. International WELL Building Institute. "WELL Building Standard."
https://www.wellcertified.com/well.

22. International WELL Building Institute. "WELL Projects." https://
www.wellcertified.com/projects.

23. The Sustainable Sites Initiative. "SITES v2 Scorecard Summary."
http://go.usgbc.org/SITES-Rating-System-and-Scoring-Card
-Thank-You.html?aliId=56869379; The Sustainable Sites Initiative.
"Certification." http://www.sustainablesites.org/certification.

24. The Sustainable Sites Initiative. http://www.sustainablesites.org/.

Case Study 3.1

Ritz Carlton Grand Cayman and Scientifically-Based Environmental Restoration

by Esteban Biondi

The Ritz Carlton Grand Cayman is a 144-acre luxury hotel property stretching from Seven Mile Beach to the North Sound on Grand Cayman Island. The property includes a 365-room hotel, a golf course, residential developments, and undeveloped land.

The Ritz Carlton property was first developed by the turn of this century. A 300-ft.-wide strip of mangroves was left along the North Sound, while the rest of the property was developed for the hotel or prepared for further development. In 2004, Hurricane Ivan caused extensive damage to the land development and to the mangrove buffer. The property owner at the time applied for permits for clearing debris (both dead trees and foreign materials brought by the storm) and building a rock berm surrounding the mangrove buffer. These actions resulted in negative impacts

Image 3.1.1 Mangrove buffer detail[1]

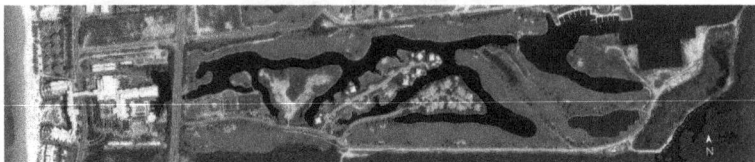

Image 3.1.2 Overall property view

to the mangroves due to interruption of water flows and modifications of the terrain elevations, which prevented natural recovery.

Ivan's damage to the resort itself also revealed deficiencies in its original coastal protection design. For instance, some of the hotel's utilities and infrastructure flooded, and a loss of power after the storm caused significantly more damage than the hurricane itself. The new owner, Five Mile Capital, undertook extensive retrofitting and improvements to the Ritz Carlton hotel and initiated an investment program to improve the hotel amenities, guest rooms, and utilities infrastructure.

In 2014, a team working for the owner put together a plan for future development of the property. This team was comprised of OBMI (land planners and architects), ATM (marina consultant, coastal engineers, and environmental consultants), Lowe Enterprises (developer), and Phoenix (a construction firm). Their experts were asked to analyze the development of new residential neighborhoods with amenities, a marina, and other resort amenities in the undeveloped eastern portions of the property.

The team proposed that future development of the Ritz Carlton property incorporate a coastal protection design based on a specific coastal study. The proposed plan included the environmental restoration of the mangrove buffer, which would be incorporated as a guest amenity. The proposed improvements included kayak trails and boardwalks through the mangroves (Fig. 3.1). This project was selected as a case study in the report entitled *Returns on Resilience: The Business Case*, prepared by the Center for Sustainability of the Urban Land Institute (ULI).[2]

The multipurpose approach to this design allowed for a solid justification from the business, coastal protection, and environmental points of view.

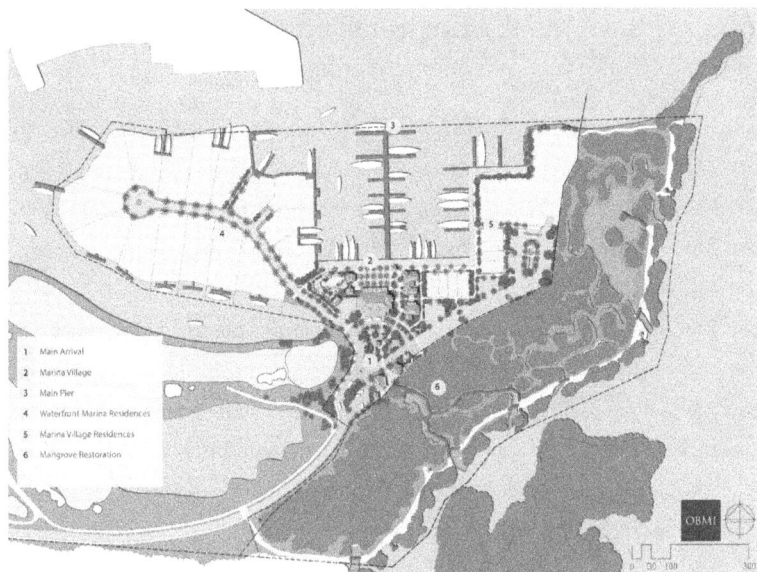

Figure 3.1 Multiple-purpose concept master plan of mangrove restoration, marina, and eastern residential area (designed by OBMI and ATM)[3]

How did this Project Incorporate Science-Based Mangrove Restoration?

After the concept was approved, the owner contracted specific mangrove studies to establish the basis for the ecological restoration strategy and design the multifunctional restoration plan. ATM conducted the biological field studies, including wetland mapping, conditions assessment, a tide studies, and also coordinated the detailed topographic survey necessary for the mangrove assessment and restoration plan. A final diagnosis of the existing conditions was completed and the environmental restoration principles were established. The environmental restoration plan was based on restoring intertidal terrain elevations and the hydraulic connection of the mangrove buffer to the ocean. In addition, the amenity feature was seamlessly included in the plan through close collaboration among architects, biologists, and engineers.

How Was the Environmental Restoration Process Managed?

The assessment and restoration plan process was coordinated with the Department of Environment of the Cayman Islands (DoE) and Jean Michele Cousteau's Ambassadors of the Environment Program (AoE)[4] at the Ritz Carlton hotel. Staff from both institutions participated in part of the fieldwork effort led by ATM staff.

The AoE runs nature-based and environmental education activities for hotel guests and community members, including kayak excursions though the area mangroves. Their professional staff was knowledgeable about the site ecology and was eager to participate in the evaluation and restoration plan. Ultimately, the AoE program will be the most important steward and user of the improved site.

The information and review process carried out with DoE exceeded the regulatory requirements at the time. DoE was pleased to have access to the developer's plans in advance, to be consulted, and to gain experience in the island's first privately promoted mangrove restoration program.

Image 3.1.3 DoE and AoE staff participated with ATM in the mangrove assessment fieldwork[5]

How Did This Project Incorporate Science-Based Coastal Protection?

Most coastal development in the Caribbean is arguably ill-prepared for the present risks of hurricane impacts. Climate change will further increase those risks in the future due to sea level rise and predicted increase in storm frequency and intensity. However, most hurricane damage occurs because presently available, science-based, coastal engineering best practices are not followed. In addition, the use of these engineering tools for sea level rise scenarios can design for future impacts.

The coastal protection analysis recommended by the team engineer included site-specific studies to evaluate present risks and future scenarios. By calculating the storm surge and wave impacts corresponding to the 100-year storm, the proposed study uses available know-how to assess hurricane risks.[6] In addition, sea level rise scenarios were proposed to take into account for shoreline design. The conceptual shoreline protection design included rock structures at different elevations and the mangrove buffer.

Will the Mangrove Restoration Provide Hurricane Protection?

The restoration of the mangrove buffer may improve marginally the protection of the landward properties, but that protection alone may not be enough. As Hurricane Ivan impacts suggest, the existing mangrove buffer does not provide enough protection from hurricane storm surge and waves. Quantitative analysis of mangrove protection under hurricane conditions is not yet fully understood by the scientific community. While there is a general confirmation that mangroves can attenuate waves, research has focused on small waves (wave height < 70 cm), and there is a need to measure the attenuation of larger wind and swell waves that may occur during hurricanes.[7] Therefore, designers had no evidence that only restoring the mangrove strip of less than 100 m will provide protection from hurricanes to future upland development.

The concept plan proposed by the design team includes maintaining part of the rock berm to induce wave breaking at the outer portion of the mangrove buffer, and designing additional reinforcement to the land-side edge of the mangrove buffer. The limited or uncertain degree of protection that may be provided by the mangroves will therefore be enhanced by rock structures to provide adequate protection to future development of the resort property. The rock revetment solution is considered resilient, as the rock structures can be readily repaired should hurricane waves and storm surge damage the coastal protection system, and can be reinforced to adapt to future conditions driven by climate change.

Lessons Learned

This case study illustrates that proactive resilience considerations by a real estate development team including coastal engineers, environmental consultants, and planners can result in innovative, multipurpose, solutions for coastal protection that maintain or restore ecological services. This design process, which is replicable in other coastal resorts, led to a design that enhanced the value of the hospitality project, and was therefore embraced by a for-profit private developer.

While this project has not been implemented yet (the property is now for sale), it is a pioneering example of a mangrove restoration project proposed by and paid for a private real estate developer as part of a high-quality resort design. This shows that smart development can meet high standards of environmental protection and restoration.

Notes

1. Image Source: Google Earth, March 2014.
2. Urban Land Institute. (2015). *Returns on Resilience: The Business Case. ULI Center for Sustainability.* Washington, D.C.: Urban Land Institute. http://uli.org/wp-content/uploads/ULI-Documents/Returns-on-Resilience-The-Business-Case.pdf.
3. Image Source: OBMI.
4. Jean-Miguel Cousteau's Ocean Futures Society. "Ambassadors of the Environment." http://www.oceanfutures.org/learning/ambassadors-environment.
5. Image Source: Greg Braun, Senior Scientist, Applied Technology & Management, Inc.

6. FEMA. (2011). *Coastal Construction Manual: Principles and Practices of Planning, Siting, Designing, Constructing, and Maintaining Residential Buildings in Coastal Areas.* 4th Edition. p.55. http://www .fema.gov/rebuild/mat/fema55.shtm.

7. Anna L. McIvor, Iris Möller, Tom Spencer, and Mark Spalding. (2012). "Reduction of Wind and Swell Waves by Mangroves," *Natural Coastal Protection Series: Report 1.* Cambridge Coastal Research Unit Working Paper 40. The Nature Conservancy and Wetlands International. http://www.naturalcoastalprotection.org/documents /reduction-of-wind-and-swell-waves-by-mangroves.

Case Study 3.2

Sugar Ridge Hotel: Inland Design as a Response to Climate Change

by Denaye Hinds

Sugar Ridge Hotel and Residences is a beautiful example of inland design at its best. This 60-room hotel, located on the western coast of Antigua, boasts gorgeous views of the ocean and neighboring islands.[1] A luxury, family-owned boutique hotel, TripAdvisor gives Sugar Ridge a 4.5 rating and lists it as a member of its Hall of Fame. While not on the beach, this hotel offers guests the same relaxing Caribbean experience made famous by seaside resorts. Utilizing its unique location in which it is constructed, the resort takes advantage of the natural assets including wide vistas and lush vegetation.

Recognizing that the beach represents significant interest to its guests, the resort is not far from the white sandy beaches of Jolly Bay and offers shuttle services to bring guests right to the ocean. In addition, activities include yoga and fitness classes, biking and walking, movies under the stars, and other nighttime entertainment. Hotel guests get the best of both worlds by having the expansive views afforded by its hillside location as well as easy access to the beach when they want it.

Sugar Ridge employs a number of internal sustainability measures that have earned the resort Green Globe certification.[2] The owners have a long-term Sustainability Management System in place that helps them

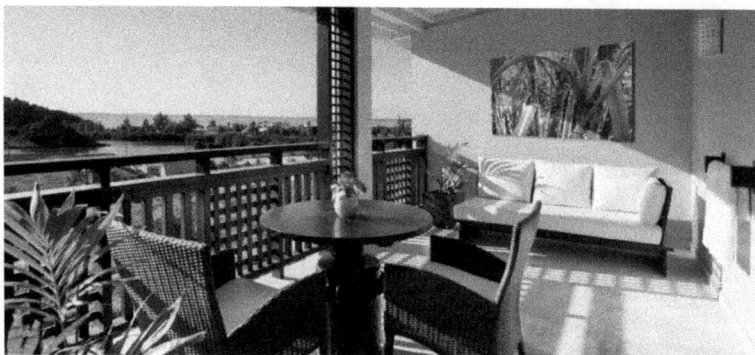

Image 3.2.1 Sugar Ridge offers rooms with a view[3]

track, measure, and improve their efforts. They attribute their success to the idea that green practices will help them sustain business for years to come. Not only does the hotel follow environmentally friendly practices within the resort, they are also active members of the community, participating in beach cleanups, volunteering with local nonprofits, and providing scholarships to students in the area.

Their most notable success in sustainability is by far their location. Buildings set back from the coast not only reduce their impact on the ocean environment, their hillside location offers protection from the increasingly fierce and erratic storms and inevitable sea level rise forecast to occur during this century. In the wake of climate change, the sea has a potential to rise over 1 m by the year 2100. This underscores the importance of siting for hotel developers in Antigua and other parts of the Caribbean.

I sat down and had a chat with one of the designers involved with Sugar Ridge, Mitch Stuart, to gauge his perspective on the role of climate change in coastal development and understand the strategies required when designing the resort. Here is how Mitch responded.

What was the inspiration behind the design of Sugar Ridge?

"This was really driven by the site itself with the contours of the property and the views to the ocean and to the hills around pretty much dictating the development layout both for the hotel and associated residences."

Image 3.2.2 Sugar Ridge rooms are built around the pool[4]

"The architectural theme is of linked pavilions which have evolved and developed further on the residential component," Stuart explained. The resort was made to contrast with the hills it was built upon. The resort's sleek lines and colors stand out from the environment in which it is nestled, providing balance between the natural and manmade landscape.

Did you encounter any site-specific challenges? If so, how did you deal with them?

Stuart listed, "Steepness of the site in some areas; rainwater run-off and control." When building a structure on a hillside location, there are many more hazards and factors that go into the construction as opposed to building on a flat terrain. The design does offer gorgeous vistas but it was not made possible without careful consideration and implementation. Sewage and drainage are also factors that need to be taken into account when considering building on a steeply sloped lot. The builders used native vegetation with secure root and stem systems to provide stabilization for slopes. This contributes to the control of speed and infiltration of rainwater runoff. Careful planning and design of appropriately spaced terraces also played a part in decreasing the runoff speed and contributed positively to enhance infiltration.

What are the main comparisons with coastal development?

"The difference with Sugar Ridge as an inland resort is the lack of a designated/owned beach club. Personally, I prefer the elevation of non-coastal development for the views and the fresher air," says the designer. What Sugar Ridge lacks in beach access they certainly make up for in other aspects of the resort. Nearly all shoreline hotels offer the same activities and opportunities to their guests. Sugar Ridge made the most of their location by offering guests the unique experience of getting more in touch with the terrestrial beauty of the island through both their spa facilities and outstanding nature walks with hotel staff. They have capitalized on their alternative location in numerous ways to combat the idea that Caribbean tourism needs to take place only on the beach.

What trends do you see in coastal resort development in the wake of climate change and sea level rise?

"Obviously design parameters have and are changing, but there doesn't appear to be a hold-back by developers on beachfront development opportunities due to climate change," comments Stuart. The reason developers are not holding back is because building by the coast has the potential to be the most profitable, short-term option. However, as more become aware of the dangers and risks associated with sea level rise and the changing climate,[5] it is possible for a change in mindset to take place. Adequate zoning and planning laws are required to ensure the diversification in development and to limit and, in some cases, prohibit development along, on, and near the shoreline. The protection of green space and shorelines present a first defense mechanism to combat storm surges and the ensuing beach erosion and should be incorporated into the governing laws for development throughout the region. Low-impact development, sustainable vegetation, vertical design, and many other principles will, if mandated, play an important role in protection of coastal and marine tourism assets.

Inland design provides opportunities for unique cultural identity and enhancing a *sense of place*. Any island may boast their offering of sea, sun, sand—the beach. However, what drives a place is its surroundings and discoveries, which can also be accessed on land and afford unique interactions with both the island's nature and local culture. This enhances the travel experience; these are the traits that are accompanied by and accomplished through inland design.

How much is a hotel's profitability based on location?

"Naturally, by not having a beachfront property potential for rates to match those which are beachfront becomes less," says Stuart. However, he explains that there is also considerable opportunity to create residential real estate and vacation home developments. The sale of these properties can help offset the lower rate of the resort. Stuart argues that "there are unique advantages and creative opportunities to enhance the tourism product outside of the usual sun, sand, and beach and provide a learning and discovery opportunity for guests and residents alike. In essence, an economically sustainable tourism model does not solely rely on the beach. As a region, diversification in the wake of climate vulnerability and increased variability of weather patterns presents the need for resilience planning for not only our siting, design, and construction, but our offerings as well."

Conclusion

Sugar Ridge Hotel is an excellent example of successful implementation of environmentally conscious siting and design. The Caribbean landscape is going to change drastically over the next century. Coastlines will be altered and millions of people's homes and livelihoods will be affected by the loss. Developers and designers should heed the current signs of climate change and take appropriate steps to innovate and incorporate resilient design solutions to protect and enhance our shorelines and coastal areas, as they contribute immensely to the survival, protection, and longevity of our people, profit, and planet.

Notes

1. Sugar Ridge Hotel and Residences. http://www.sugarridgeantigua.com/.
2. Green Globe. (2016). "Do Good by Always Doing Better." http://greenglobe.com/.
3. Image Source: Sugar Ridge Hotel and Residences.
4. Image Source: Sugar Ridge Hotel and Residences.
5. Caribbean Community Climate Change Centre. (2014). "Sea Level Rise," http://caribbeanclimate.bz/featured-articles/sea-level-rise.html.

Case Study 3.3
Via Verde: USGBC Guidelines and Principles

by Denaye Hinds

The Project Site

Via Verde, which means *green way*, is a development that is part of a larger objective to revitalize the South Bronx area in New York City. This sustainable and affordable mixed-use development focused on promoting a healthy, urban lifestyle, also offers innovative solutions applicable to the Caribbean.

Via Verde originated in a design competition held by the city of New York and the local chapter of the American Institute of Architects. The project includes 222 residential units, 7,500 sq. ft. of commercial space, and 40,000 sq. ft. of *green* roof and additional open green space (Fig. 3.2). Built on a *brownfield*, the nearly US$99 million project provides community members with an economically sustainable opportunity to rent or own units in a healthy environment. With health and wellness becoming

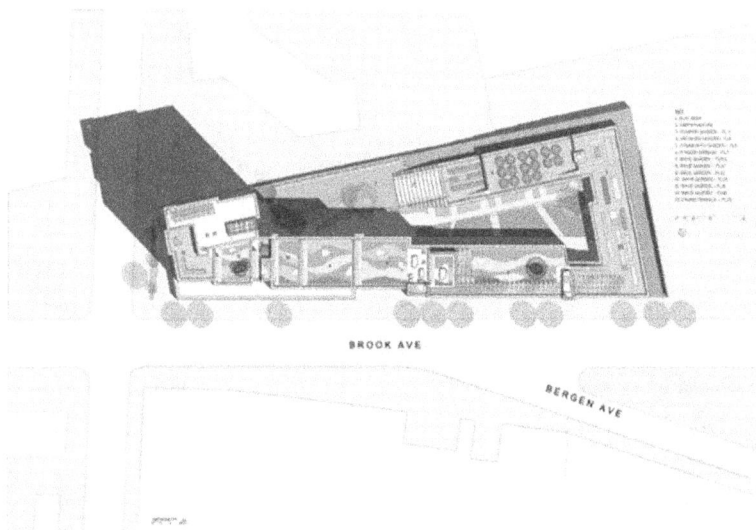

Figure 3.2 Via Verde Site Map[1]

a large part of the focus in developing communities, the project aimed to tackle specific issues such as childhood obesity and asthma.

Despite the location of the project, the context is compelling and the siting, design, architecture, and construction principles by which the project stands are relevant as well to the Caribbean. There is a gap in the socio-economic spectrum of developments throughout the Caribbean. It is imperative now, more than ever, that mixed-use developments encompass specific elements that benefit not only the developers and the typically foreign occupants, but also the surrounding local community and the island as a whole.

As in New York, suitable land is a premium on most islands. Siting and location play an important role, with limited land mass and threatening sea level rise, looking at opportunities to redevelop and enhance existing sites, reducing sprawl, and limiting virgin land development close to the shoreline are avenues to be taken into account when siting a development.

Under the U.S. Green Building Council's LEED criteria,[2] developments should ideally be located in areas close to existing infrastructure and communities in order to lessen their development footprint. LEED criteria also require there be paths to conserve species and ecological communities, that coastal and marine developments must undergo studies beyond simple environmental impact analysis (EIA) requirements, and that there must be standards and studies that outline the intended impacts of the development over time to ensure responsible tourism asset projects.

Materials and Resources, Energy and Air Quality

The Via Verde project's goal was to fuse together nature and city. The site, a 1.5 acre triangular block, posed some degree of complexity in order to maximize outdoor as well as interior space. According to an Urban Land Institute (ULI) case study of Via Verde, "The development makes the most of its narrow, triangular site, with three building types that step up from three stories at the southern end of the site to a 20-story tower at the northern end. The buildings are oriented to the south to take advantage of views afforded by the adjacent permanent open space . . . and to maximize solar gain."[3]

In terms of aesthetics and function, one of the most significant aspects of the project are the large green roofs that cascade down from the 20-story

Image 3.3.1 Green Roofs on Via Verde[4]

high rise to the lower level townhouses. The terraced roofs also play host to a variety of fruit and vegetable gardens that can be used by the community as a fresh, healthy food source. The green roofs help reduce heat and energy use as well as reducing water runoff and providing redirection of storm water, all of which lessens the strain on municipal resources. And the roofs afford residents access to nature in the middle of the city.

In designing for climate, energy reduction plays a huge role. Design characteristics to encourage energy independence, passive design elements, and clean energy sources assist in reducing CO_2 emissions. Energy saving practices employed at Via Verde include solar panels on the southern side of the building that produce enough energy to power all lights in common areas. Each individual unit has Energy Star[5] appliances, which use less electricity, efficient lighting, operable windows, water conserving plumbing, and sunshades to reduce the need for air conditioning.

Solar panels have been criticized in the past for their high purchase and maintenance costs and relative lack of aesthetic, functionality, and wind resistance. However, technology has improved over the years and the cost of solar is steadily decreasing worldwide. The many advances offered by the solar and battery storage industry include integrated building and roof systems, white-colored panels (for aesthetic purposes), *kirigami-inspired*[iii] solar panels[6] whose cells can turn so that they always face the sun, and, more recently, technology that allows the *skin* of a building to be transformed into a solar energy source. Michigan State University research teams are experimenting with fully transparent solar cells (transparent luminescent solar concentrators) that may have the ability to turn every glass window into a power source.[7]

According to the ULI case study of Via Verde, "Windows are large and operable, allowing more light into the units, as well as better ventilation and higher air quality. Balconies and sunshades add interest as well as function. Solar panels, angled to catch the sun's rays, are used as part of the building skin on the southern exposure."[8] The latter allows for the design to incorporate indoor air quality and energy conservation. High-tech rain screens deflect water from the building and minimize water vapor and infiltration, lowering the costs of maintenance and reducing the risk of mold and mildew.

With climate variability, it is imperative to understand not only design and construction, but also how occupants fair within these structures. For instance, consideration of how ventilation and materials used affect indoor air quality plays an important role in determining the comfort the buildings' occupants.

For the Caribbean, material selection and location contribute to the carbon created during the design and construction processes. Sourcing materials locally rather than importing them, and determining how they will be constructed once available on island are important topics within the discussion of sustainable, resilient climate strategies. In the case of Via Verde, "the large prefabricated sections were made locally, on [nearby] Long Island. Highly insulated, the panels added points toward certification under the LEED program. The use of prefabricated panels also allowed quicker construction and a tighter, more impervious building envelope."[9] The interiors were designed to bring in as much natural light as possible and utilize cross-ventilation in order to reduce energy costs. Floor tiles are made of renewable resources, bamboo and ceramic, to lessen the environmental impact, and they are free of toxins that could harm residents.

[iii] Kirigami is an ancient Japanese paper-folding art.

In the Caribbean, tourism assets located near the coast have an added concern of saltwater intrusion, rust, humidity, mold, and mildew. Therefore, material selection and air quality must be carefully considered. Locally sourced interior items made with bio-based and recycled content may provide options; however, the life cycle analysis and off-gas potential are factors that must also be considered when evaluating materials. Adequate air quality management systems, which include monitoring of CO_2 levels and air purification specific to the region, should be put in place to ward off harmful effects on occupants and interior materials.

Healthy Living and Active Design

Via Verde has achieved LEED Gold certification[10] and exceeds Enterprise Green standards for environmental responsibility.[11] This means they have put sustainable and healthy practices at the forefront of their design. In fact, over 20 percent of the materials used in construction included recycled materials, and over 80 percent of the waste was recycled after project completion. To save water, a storm water reclamation system was put in place and used for irrigation of the green roofs. It is even more urgent for Caribbean coastal developments, which are increasingly susceptible to storm surges, to put in place adequate infrastructure support.

The Via Verde development also employs active design techniques that encourage residents to take the stairs, spend time outdoors, and actively engage in all of the building's amenities. All stairways have bright windows and motion sensors to ensure that lights are only on when needed. Walkability is also a huge component to the Via Verde project. It is easy walking distance to transport (buses and trains), businesses, a public school, a grocery store, and Yankee Baseball Stadium. There is also bike storage to encourage use of alternative transportation and reduce CO_2 emissions and a fitness center and gym to enable residents to maintain a fitness regime.

This type of *active design* is not as yet often found within the Caribbean, but this is beginning to change. These concepts clearly complement tourism and health and wellness centers together with spa and yoga are becoming increasingly popular as niche products. In addition, active design principles are beginning to be embedded within the architecture of tourism offerings in an effort to both increase the health of guests and more readily achieve responsible design.

Via Verde serves as a model for not only housing developers in urban areas but also for coastal complexes of condos, hotels, commercial, and general mixed-use developments. The Via Verde project has proved financially feasible, won critical acclaim, and been successful in the market. It offers a new perspective on how design can be achieved in a more creative, attractive, and sustainable manner, in the South Bronx as well as in the Caribbean.

Notes

1. Figure Source: Phipps/Rose/Dattner/Grimshaw.
2. U.S. Green Building Council. (2016). *LEED v4 for Neighborhood Development*. http://www.usgbc.org/sites/default/files/LEED%20v4 %20ND_04.05.16_current.pdf.
3. Urban Land Institute. (January 22, 2014). "ULI Case Studies: *Via Verde Design*." Matkins. http://uli.org/case-study/uli-case-studies-via-verde/
4. Image Source: Marilyn Bontempo/Mid-Hudson Marketing.
5. Energy Star. https://www.energystar.gov/.
6. Michigan News. (2015). *Inspired by Art, Lightweight Solar Cells Track the Sun*. Video. University of Michigan. http://ns.umich.edu /new/multimedia/videos/23109-inspired-by-art-lightweight-solar -cells-track-the-sun.
7. MSU Today. (2014). "Solar Energy that Doesn't Block the View." Michigan State University. http://msutoday.msu.edu/news/2014 /solar-energy-that-doesnt-block-the-view/.
8. Urban Land Institute. (2014).
9. Urban Land Institute. (2014).
10. U.S. Green Building Council. "Via Verde/The Green Way: LEED Scorecard." http://www.usgbc.org/projects/verde-green-way.
11. Enterprise. "2015 Green Communities Criteria." http://www .enterprisecommunity.com/solutions-and-innovation/enterprise -green-communities/criteria.

CHAPTER 4

Coastal Hotels and Resorts

Overview—Climate Change and Coastal Resorts and Hotels

Denaye Hinds

The Caribbean has more than 2,600 hotels[1] with approximately 225,000 hotel rooms in 2015,[2] and of those about 226 are all-inclusive resorts.[3] While the large international all-inclusive and branded resorts—Sandals, Marriott, Hilton, Four Seasons, Riu, Melia, Barcelo, and so forth—dominate the advertising and, together with the major cruise lines, are typically the public face of Caribbean tourism, the small, independent, and boutique hotels make up the majority of accommodations. These boutique accommodations play an important role in offering character, charm, culture, and an authentic Caribbean experience, particularly to the more discerning travel customers. The unique models by which they operate, the level of local knowledge and entrepreneurship they create, and the contribution to diversification of the tourism offering is undisputed. The 2015 Survey of Wealth and Affluence, conducted by YouGov and Time Inc., shows that "since 2007, affluent travelers who favor a luxury hotel brand has declined by 81 percent, today only 15 percent are brand loyal,"[4] thus reinforcing the strength of the boutique and independent hotels within the Caribbean's tourism sector.

Tourism is the Caribbean's leading industry and, in 2015, the pace of growth of Caribbean tourism outperformed every other major region in the world for the first time ever.[5] The main source markets for travel into the Caribbean continue to be, as in past years, the United States and

Europe, followed by Canada. With U.S. spending in leisure travel set to increase by 15.9 percent globally, the demand for travel is continuously on the rise, with the Caribbean being the second most popular destination for U.S. travelers, after Europe.[6] According to *Travel + Leisure* magazine, the top three factors luring tourists to the Caribbean are: (1) scenery and landscape, (2) climate and weather, and (3) hotel and resort options.[7]

Impacts of Climate Change on Coastal Resorts and Hotels

With a region so heavily dependent upon tourism and most tourism concentrated in low-lying coastal zones, Caribbean hotels and resorts are particularly vulnerable to adverse occurrences linked to and exacerbated by climate change. While the Caribbean nations contribute less than 1 percent to total greenhouse gas emissions, they are expected to be among the earliest to suffer an outsized impact from climate change, with sea level rise (SLR), hotter temperatures, and extreme weather events all increasing.

According to the CARICOM Task Force on Climate Change, 28 million of the 40 million people in the Caribbean live in coastal cities, towns, and villages. "With a 2°C increase, 1300 sq. km of land will disappear in the Caribbean by the end of this century: an area comparable to the whole of Barbados, Saint-Vincent and the Grenadines, Anguilla, Antigua and Barbuda, combined."[8] CARICOM researchers estimate that with a 2°C rise in global temperature, the socioeconomic consequences for the Caribbean will be devastating: 150 tourism resorts, 21 airports, and five power plants would be lost or damaged; land surrounding 35 seaports would be flooded; 567 km of roads would be lost; and more than 110,000 Caribbean people would be displaced.

The Caribbean is already experiencing the adverse effects of climate change: SLR has become more evident in recent years, storm intensity and severity has increased, and there have been several severe multi-year droughts in recent history. While Caribbean countries have long planned for the annual hurricane season, the increasing frequency, ferocity, and unpredictability of these tropical storms is challenging disaster management and rebuilding efforts. For example, the financial losses from Hurricane Erika in August 2015 to Dominica were estimated to be

US$483 million, with over US$30 million in damage and destruction to the tourism sector alone. Total damage was equivalent to 90 percent of Dominica's gross domestic product (GDP).[9]

Annual average losses from wind, storm surge, and inland flooding are estimated to be as high as 6 percent of GDP in some countries in the Caribbean, and climate change has the potential to increase these risks by 33 to 50 percent, by 2030. One study found that if no action is taken, increased hurricane damages, loss of tourism revenue, and infrastructure damages in the Caribbean could total US$22 billion a year by 2050 and US$46 billion by 2100.[10]

In the wake of climate change, new natural disasters and initially unexplainable events are occurring. Most recently, coastal hotels and communities in the Caribbean have already been facing one such phenomenon: Sargassum. With little to no warning, the massive influx of Sargassum seaweed has rendered many beaches unpleasant, uninhabitable, and inaccessible. This has led to reduced bookings and cancellations, closures of beachfront property, dramatically increased daily costs for removal and beach cleanup, cancellations of tours and ocean-based activities near the beach shores/coastlines, beach erosion, and other adverse impacts on shorelines. Hotels have lost revenue and been forced to lay off staff. In addition, fishing communities, which supply fresh food to coastal resorts, are also suffering from the Sargassum epidemic.

Coastal Hotels Address Climate Change

Even though tourism's carbon footprint in the Caribbean is relatively minor on a global scale, it still needs to be addressed. Both hotel construction and operations contribute to greenhouse gas (GHG) emissions. New construction, for instance, contributes to emissions through the alteration of landmass. It is estimated that nearly 250 m^2 of land is used for every bed in a hotel, including for built infrastructure, parking, and landscaping. In addition, 20 kg of CO_2 is used—emitted into the atmosphere—per night per guest bed for the lighting, air conditioning, and heating systems of hotels.[11] Therefore, the business-as-usual operations of both small, independent hotels as well as large or all-inclusive resorts are contributing to the atmosphere's warming.

Fortunately, many Caribbean hotels are working in a range of ways to decrease their carbon footprints. There are a number of organizations in the Caribbean that are helping to provide sustainable technologies and are promoting eco-certification programs. Table 4.1 summarizes the third party eco-certification programs that are currently in use in the Caribbean. As indicated, many of these certification programs contain criteria addressing climate change. In addition, the Global

Table 4.1 Eco-Certification and Eco-Labeling Programs in Use in the Caribbean[12]

Certification program [13]	Criteria	Caribbean countries with certified hotels
Biosphere Responsible Tourism (IRT)	Environmental, Socio/ cultural, Economic, Climate change	Dominican Republic, Mexico
EarthCheck	Environmental, Socio/ cultural, Economic, Climate change	Antigua, The Bahamas, Barbados, Dominican Republic, Grenada, Jamaica, Mexico, Saint Lucia
Travelife	Environmental, Socio/ cultural	Aruba, The Bahamas, Barbados, Costa Rica, Curacao, Dominican Republic, Jamaica, Mexico
Rainforest Alliance	Environmental, Socio/ cultural, Economic, Climate change	Belize, Dominican Republic, Ecuador, Guadeloupe, Jamaica, Martinique, Mexico
Distintivo S	Environmental, Socio/ cultural, Economic	Mexico
Green Globe	Environmental, Socio/ cultural, Economic, Climate change	Antigua, Antigua and Barbuda, Aruba, Barbados, Belize, Bermuda, BVI, Cayman Islands, Dominican Republic, Grenada, Guadalupe, Jamaica, Martinique, Mexico, Puerto Rico, St. Lucia
Tourism Environmental Quality	Environmental	Mexico

Table 4.1 Eco-Certification and Eco-Labeling Programs in Use in the Caribbean (continued)

Green Key	Environmental	Dominican Republic, Mexico, Martinique, Puerto Rico, Sint Maarten
Green Key Global	Environmental, Socio/ cultural, Economic, Climate change	Barbados, Mexico
Green Hotels Global	Environmental, Climate change	Barbados
TripAdvisor GreenLeaders	Environmental	Throughout the Caribbean
Great Green Deal—CERTIFICA	Environmental, Socio/ cultural, Economic, Climate change	Dominican Republic, Guatemala
Sustainable Riviera Maya	Environmental, Socio/ cultural, Economic	Mexico
Skyviews Sustainability Awards	Environmental, Climate change	Bonaire, Dominica, Grenada, St. Kitts and Nevis, St. Lucia
LEED	Environmental, Climate change	Aruba, Jamaica, Puerto Rico
ISO 14001	Environmental, Economic, Climate change	The Bahamas, Barbados, Cuba, Dominican Republic, Jamaica, Trinidad and Tobago

Sustainable Tourism Council (GSTC) has to date conducted comprehensive sustainability assessments of three Caribbean destinations—St. Kitts, Cayman Islands, and Riviera Maya, Mexico—and this provides an important diagnostic tool that can help a destination to prepare for full certification.

While third party certification programs are not widely adopted in the Caribbean, most of the region's resort brands have internal sustainability policies that reduce use and costs of fossil fuel-based energy, water, and other resources, and many of these good practices also help to reduce GHG emissions and counter climate change impacts. The following is a brief description of sustainability policies that have been put in place by two of the leading hotel brands that are prominent in the Caribbean:

starwood
Hotels and Resorts

Image 4.0.1 © *Starwood Hotels and Resorts*

Starwood

Starwood, which was officially acquired by Marriott beginning in 2016,[i] had 16 hotels in the Caribbean and was the first US hotel company with authorization to operate in Cuba.[14] Starwood's sustainability program has set target goals of a 30 percent reduction in energy, a 20 percent reduction in water consumption, and a 30 percent reduction in GHG emissions per built hotel room by 2020[15] (Case Study 4.1). This is amplified by its Carbon Disclosure Project, which measures and reports on GHG emissions, water management, and climate change strategies in all properties owned, managed, and franchised by Starwood. Through the company's Global Citizenship Intranet, associates have online access to a number of tools, including "how to focus on sustainable food and beverage, provide guests and meeting planners with their carbon footprint using the Hotel Carbon Measurement Initiative, view LEED and green building roadmaps, and participate in waste minimization programs such as Clean The World." Starwood's Supplier Code of Conduct, established in 2015, promotes localized, organic, and Fair Trade food and beverages, while its *Make a Green Choice* program allows guests to decline full housekeeping for up to three days in a row in exchange for rewards points or food and beverage vouchers.[16]

---

[i] As first announced on November 16, 2015, Starwood entered into a definitive merger agreement with Marriott International, Inc. under which Marriott would acquire Starwood in a stock and cash transaction. The transaction closed in late 2016 at which time the Starwood name no longer was used.

Sandals

THE LUXURY INCLUDED' VACATION

Image 4.0.2 © Sandals Hotels & Resorts

Sandals

Sandals Resorts, the Caribbean's leading locally owned chain, has 15 properties.[17] Sandals first gained recognition for its environmental programs in 1997, when Sandals Negril Beach Resort & Spa in Jamaica became Green Globe certified. Its current environmental programs are governed by Sandals' Earth Guard Policy, which includes programs on staff awareness training, water conservation, energy management, waste management, control of hazardous substances, and working with responsible local suppliers. All Sandals resorts participate in the EarthCheck benchmarking and certification program,[18] and the Environmental Health and Safety manager at each resort is EarthCheck Coordinator Certified.[19]

The success of Sandals' initiatives became apparent, for instance, during the 2011–2012 season, when the company's average water usage per night dropped from 1,177 liters to 776 liters—a drop of 34 percent—through water recycling, rain, and well water harvesting. Efficiency initiatives and energy usage per night was cut from 189 mega joules per night to 163 per night. Sandals achieved this 14 percent reduction through reengineering doors and windows, solar heating in pools, and *intelligent* thermostats that adjust lighting and temperature based on occupancy.[20]

Independent Hotels

For independent hotels, one of the most important resources is the Caribbean Alliance for Sustainable Tourism (CAST),[21] headquartered in Miami. Founded in 1997 as part of the Caribbean Hotel and Tourism Association (CHTA), CAST's mission is to provide guidelines and criteria for hotels to help them to operate more sustainably.

Image 4.0.3 © CAST/CHTA

While CAST declined in capacity over the last decade, it has recently been revitalized with the following strategic focus:

- **Information and Resources**: To provide detailed studies, lessons learned from the best and the worst practices, information, and resources to make the case for sustainability.
- **Cooperation and Collaboration:** To work in partnership with countries, public and private sector stakeholders, aligned groups and organizations throughout the region and internationally.
- **Research:** To conduct and collaborate in developing primary research and collating secondary research on sustainability.
- **Advocacy:** To promote responsible environmental and social issues and practices within the Caribbean tourism sector and the broader business community, the public sector, the general public, and to contribute to and influence governance and decision-making regarding sustainability within the sector.
- **Sustainability Training and Special Projects**: To provide toolkits, resource guides, training programs, and modules.

CAST is continuing its mission as the regional Caribbean body that provides tools to assist tourism enterprises with sustainable development and operations and serves as the private tourism sector's collective voice for sustainable practices.

Another resource for independent hotels is Caribbean Hotel Energy Efficiency and Renewable Energy Action (CHENACT), an energy efficiency program based in Barbados and financed by international agencies and the Barbados government.[22] The objective of CHENACT is to improve the competitiveness of small and medium-sized hotels (defined as less than 400 rooms) in the Caribbean through better use of energy, with the emphasis on renewable energy and micro-generation (Case Study 4.4).

Climate Friendly Initiatives by Resorts and Hotels

Today the Caribbean is dotted with both boutique hotels and international resort brands that are addressing, in a variety of ways, the challenges of sustainability and climate change. Increasingly, hotels are installing solar panels and taking other measures to reduce energy costs and GHG emissions. By 2014, the largest solar resort in the Caribbean was the 317-room Westin Dawn Beach Resort & Spa on St. Maarten. Its 2,602 solar panels with a 755-kilowatt capacity has the ability to channel six to eight hours of solar energy daily throughout the resort, while reducing CO_2 emissions by 1.9 million pounds annually.[23]

While the size of this solar installation is impressive, there are smaller programs, successful technology integrations, and alternative resource

Image 4.0.4 Solar panels on Westin Dawn Beach Resort & Spa, St. Maarten[24]

initiatives throughout the region to reduce dependence on fossil fuels. And the resources and technologies are gradually becoming more widely available to all the island states.

Some independent hotels find ways to reduce electricity consumption through passive design techniques. Whether as a renovation, addition, or new build, designing with an emphasis on cross-ventilation, trade winds, and taking advantage of location and passive design techniques assist significantly in reducing a hotel's energy costs and GHG emissions. A few of the independent resorts that have mastered this technique include Jade Mountain, Anse Chastenet, and Fond Doux Plantation & Resort in St. Lucia and Sugar Ridge Hotel in Antigua and Barbuda (Case Study 3.2).

In the wake of climate change, freshwater, for both potable and nonpotable uses, is increasingly scarce, particularly in coastal regions. With sea level rise (SLR), salt water is intruding into aquifers and low-lying rivers, streams, and freshwater supplies, and tourism and coastal communities are competing for limited water supplies. Damage and destruction of tourism infrastructure, ports, marinas, and beachfront properties, potential backups from drainage systems, reduction and loss of mangroves and other wetlands that naturally buffer and assist with healthy water and land-based ecosystems can be compromised with SLR. The Ritz Carlton Cayman has employed several resilience techniques along its sea front in an effort to ensure sustainability. Concrete walls and removable flood protection walls surround their generators, preventing storm water and flooding. However, the key resilience feature will be the restored mangrove that will help provide an environmentally sensitive storm protection system (Case Study 3.1).[25]

Waste management and conscious efforts to buy locally, where applicable, reduce packaging, and utilize alternative disposal methods are increasingly adding to the efforts to reduce emissions and negative water impacts. Many hotels are seeking alternatives to plastic water bottles and are looking at the Natura system[26] and atmospheric water generator systems for potable water supplies in bars, rooms, and restaurants. A growing number of hotels, including Bucuti & Tara Resort in Aruba, provide guests with reusable water bottles in order to stop use of plastic bottles (Case Study 4.2).

Several islands, including St. Lucia and Bermuda, have banned plastic bags, while some hotels in Grenada have been lobbying against use of Styrofoam containers. Responsible sourcing methods and sustainable purchasing techniques also can help to limit waste generation. The key is not only to have an environmental purchasing policy, but to share it with local and overseas vendors in an effort to educate and encourage businesses throughout the supply chain.

Uncontrolled burning of waste, hazardous fires that originate from improper landfilling operations, and poor waste collection all plague island nations. While most islands still lack effective recycling systems, Punta Cana, the leading tourism destination in the Dominican Republic, has developed a large-scale recycling and waste management facility that services the area's resorts, vacation homes, and the international airport (Case Study 4.3).

While hoteliers recognize energy as both a major financial cost and contributor of GHG emissions, a range of other factors help determine the carbon footprint and climate change resilience of a coastal hotel. These include where and how the hotel is built, the choice of materials and technologies, and use of locally produced products. In addition, efforts to reduce sprawl and promote low-impact development, establish waste-free and reduced waste purchasing policies, set requirements for resilience in design, and responsibility in operations, all help coastal hotels and resorts to both reduce the negative impacts and to withstand storms, surges, and rising sea levels. But effective implementation of these requires shifts in thinking, vision, design, and operations. The great news is that there are organizations, experts, and early adopter hotels willing to lead the charge and embrace the challenge. The Center for Responsible Travel's documentary film, *Caribbean 'Green' Travel: Your Choices Make a Difference,* portrays the best practices of a number of sustainable coastal tourism resorts in Grenada, Aruba, Jamaica, and the Dominican Republic.[27]

Caribbean-wide Climate Change Initiatives

Over the years, there have been larger projects designed to address climate change more broadly in the Caribbean, and not simply within the tourism industry. For example, the Caribbean Planning for Adaptation to Climate Change (CPACC) project,[28] which ran from 1997 to 2001, was implemented by the World Bank and executed by the Organization of American States (OAS). CPACC's goal was to build capacity in the Caribbean for the adaptation to climate change impacts, particularly SLR, through vulnerability assessments, adaptation planning, and capacity building activities. Participating countries included most CARICOM members: Antigua and Barbuda, The Bahamas, Barbados, Belize, Dominica, Grenada, Guyana, Jamaica, Saint Lucia, St. Kitts and Nevis, St. Vincent, and Trinidad and Tobago.

The World Bank's Adaptation to Climate Change in the Caribbean (ACCC) Project,[29] succeeded the CPACC project and ran from 2001 to 2004. ACCC's outcomes for CARICOM countries included: developing guidelines to assist in integrating climate change in the EIA process, launching a master's program in climate change, and developing and disseminating risk management guidelines for climate change adaptation decision-making.

Through the work of projects and institutions such as those described above, today both branded resort chains and small independent hotels have access to more robust and less technical information and tools to assist in addressing climate change. However, despite this progress, there remains some disconnect between information and implementation. As the July 2015 Think Tank on Climate Change and Coastal and Marine

Image 4.0.5 Beach erosion in Negril, Jamaica[30]

Tourism, hosted by CREST and the Puntacana Ecological Foundation, revealed, Caribbean resorts and vacation homes continue to be built on or very near the beach, rather than observing sufficient setbacks based on climate change and SLR forecasts.[31]

Individual Islands Seek to Reduce Dependence on Fossil Fuel

Alongside Caribbean-wide climate change initiatives that are helping the tourism sector to reduce its carbon footprint, several islands have also set goals to reduce dependence on fossil fuels and transition to alternative energy sources. These initiatives will benefit coastal hotels that will be able to secure their energy from these alternative sources. Rapid transition from centralized energy systems based on fossil fuels to those based on a mix of locally distributed and locally appropriate renewable energy resources is viewed by many as the most effective means of mitigating and adapting to climate change.[32]

For instance, in 2014 Virgin founder Sir Richard Branson's climate group, the Carbon War Room (CWR), partnered with the Rocky Mountain Institute (RMI) to create the Ten Island Challenge to encourage alternative energy through using the islands' abundant supply of sun and wind. The challenge is working with the Caribbean nations to create ambitious renewable energy plans and targets, and to build the necessary infrastructure and resource capacity. Aruba was the first nation to join the challenge, and by late 2015, St. Lucia, Grenada, the British Virgin Islands, The Bahamas, Turks and Caicos, San Andres, Providencia, and Belize had all joined as well. [33]

The Dutch island of Aruba, which has set the ambitious goal of being fully fossil energy independent by 2020, has made a number of investments in clean energy and in sun and wind power. By 2015, Aruba's public transportation system had become completely electric, thereby eliminating all GHG emissions from its buses and other vehicles. In addition, the island has enhanced its energy storage capacity by utilizing grid-scale technology, has built a wind turbine park that provides 30 percent of the island's energy, and has installed a solar panel park on the roof of the airport parking lot.[34]

Another Dutch island, Bonaire, has also made plans to reach the goal of generating 100 percent of its electricity from renewable sources. By early 2016, Bonaire had installed 12 wind turbines with a capacity of 11 megawatts. These generate on average 40 to 45 percent of the island's electricity, and at peak wind times can contribute up to 90 percent of the island's electricity needs. In addition, batteries permit this electricity to be stored for use in times of low wind.[35]

Other islands are joining the renewables bandwagon. Due to high fuel costs and favorable *feed-in tariffs* (a policy mechanism designed to accelerate investment in renewable energy technologies), the French island of Guadeloupe has reached 30 percent solar power penetration, which puts it on par with Germany. In January 2014, BMR Energy announced financing for 36 megawatts of wind power in Jamaica at a cost of US$63 million, which will directly offset diesel purchases.[36]

In Cuba, which is emerging as a rapidly growing tourism hotspot, renewable energy capacity has also been growing. In 2012, the government announced plans to invest US$3.5 billion to increase its renewable energy capacity to 24 percent by 2030. To achieve this goal, Cuba is looking to expand its renewable energy technologies as well as increase its energy-efficiency, energy-savings, and energy storage programs. In 2015, Cuba's Minister of Energy and Mines, Alfredo Lopez announced plans to build 13 new wind facilities, adding to the four existing facilities. In addition, Cuba plans to convert its aging power plants from oil burning to much cleaner natural gas.[37]

Conclusion

For every climate-related challenge, there is, it seems, a solution. As a region, the Caribbean has the ability to redesign the tourism sector and diversify in the wake of climate change and SLR. Despite the negative impacts and scarcity of resources, climate change is also offering a turning point, an opportunity to reconsider how we value our resources and how we can aggressively and creatively adapt to the changing climate realities. To overcome these challenges, we must respect our coastal and marine environments, site and design hotels to withstand increased storms and SLR, actively reduce and reuse, and instill and implement behavioral changes and conservation techniques. Climate change and SLR provide a unique opportunity to learn from failures and foster a fresh and innovate era of repurposing, resilience, sustainability, and diversity. The ability to network and partner with other nations and among tourism businesses to meet the needs of our future generations without compromising our current resources is an exceptional task, one which will undoubtedly change the landscape of how we design, develop, and operate coastal resorts to meet the new realities. Going forward, our mantra must be: Sustain, Elevate, Innovate.

Notes

1. Loreto Duffy-Mayers, Regional Program Manager, Caribbean Hotel Energy Efficiency and Renewable Energy Action (CHENACT). (2015). Email interview. Barbados.

2. Parris Jordan. (November 2015). "Three Key Takeaways." *2015 CHICOS.HVS Caribbean Hotel Investment Conference and Operations Summit.* Puerto Rico.

3. Le Beach Club. (2015). "Master List of All-Inclusive Resorts." http://www.lebeachclub.com/MasterList.html.

4. Nathan Lump. (October 2015). *Travel + Leisure* Presentation at Caribbean Hospitality Industry Exchange Forum (CHIEF). Puerto Rico.

5. Hugh Riley, Secretary General, Caribbean Tourism Organization. (February 16, 2016). "State of the Tourism Industry Report." Caribbean Tourism Organization.

6. Nathan Lump. (October 2015).

7. Nathan Lump. (October 2015).

8. CARICOM Task Force on Climate Change. (2015). http://www.1point5.info/8-facts.

9. Government of the Commonwealth of Dominica. (September 25, 2015). *Rapid Damage and Impact Assessment Tropical Storm Erika – August 27, 2015.* p.18. http://www.drrinacp.org/sites/drrinacp.org/files/publication/Commonwealth percent20of percent20Dominica percent20- percent20Rapid percent20Damage percent20and percent20Needs percent20Assessment percent20Final percent20Report percent20.pdf.

10. Murray Simpson, Daniel Scott, and Ulric Trotz. (2011). *Climate Change's Impact on the Caribbean's Ability to Sustain Tourism, Natural Assets, and Livelihood*. Inter-American Development Bank Environmental, Safeguards Unit, Technical Notes No. IDB-TN-23. http://www.uncclearn.org/sites/default/files/inventory/idb14.pdf.

11. Stefan Gössling. (December 2002). "Global Environmental Consequences of Tourism." *Global Environmental Change*, 12(4). pp. 283-302 http://www.sciencedirect.com/science/article/pii/S0959378002000444.

12. Rae-Gean Jenkins, who holds a MES in tourism policy and planning and is a tourism consultant based in St. Kitts, researched this table. Compiled by Helena Servé, research assistant at the Center for Responsible Travel.

13. The following are the websites for the programs listed in this Table. Biosphere Responsible Tourism (IRT): www.biospheretourism.com/en; Earthcheck: earthcheck.org/; Travelife: www.travelife.org/Hotels/landing_page.asp; Rainforest Alliance: www.rainforest-alliance.org/business/marketing/marks/certified; Distintivo S: www.gob.mx/sectur/acciones-y-programas/programa-de-calidad-distintivo-s; Green Globe: greenglobe.com/; Green Key: www.greenkey.global/; Green Key Global: greenkeyglobal.com/; Green Hotels Global: www.greenhotelsglobal.com/; TripAdvisor GreenLeaders: www.tripadvisor.com/GreenLeaders; Great Green Deal CERTI-FICA: www.sellosverdes.com/; Sustainable Riviera Maya: www.rivieramayasostenible.org/; Skyviews Awards: bluegreenmatters.org/about/; LEED: www.usgbc.org/leed; ISO 14001: www.iso.org/iso/iso14000.

14. Starwood. "Resort Directory." http://www.starwoodhotels.com/resorts/directory/hotels/all/list.html?sortType=region.

15. Starwood. "Global Citizenship–Sustainability." http://www.starwoodhotels.com/corporate/about/citizenship/sustainability/index.html.

16. Starwood. "Global Citizenship–Sustainability Programs & Initiatives." http://www.starwoodhotels.com/corporate/about/citizenship/sustainability/programs.html.

17. Sandals. "The Sandals Resorts." http://www.sandals.com/destinations/.

18. Sandals. "Earthguard." http://www.sandals.com/difference/eco-friendly -resorts.cfm.

19. Tiffany Mullins. (2013). "Sandals Earth Guard: Eco-Friendly Practices at Luxury Resorts." http://biofriendly.com/blog/green-ideas/eco -friendly/sandals-earth-guard-eco-friendly-practices-at-luxury -resorts/

20. Tiffany Mullins. (2013).

21. Caribbean Hotel & Tourism Association. "CAST." http://www .caribbeanhotelandtourism.com/cast/.

22. CHENACT. "Creating Sustainable Tourism for the Caribbean." http://www.chenact.com/.

23. Elaine Glusac. (2014). "A Caribbean Resort Goes Solar." In Transit blog, *New York Times*. http://intransit.blogs.nytimes.com/2014/04 /11/a-caribbean-resort-goes-solar/?_r=0.

24. Image Source: Sollega Inc.

25. Urban Land Institute (2015). *Returns on Resilience: The Business Case*. ULI Center for Sustainability. Washington, D.C.: Urban Land Institute. pp. 27-29. http://uli.org/wp-content/uploads/ULI-Documents/Returns-on-Resilience-The-Business-Case.pdf.

26. Natura Water System. http://www.naturawater.com/.

27. *Caribbean 'Green' Travel: Your Choices Make a Difference*. (2016). Documentary film. Center for Responsible Travel. www.responsibletravel.org.

28. Caribbean Community Secretariat. "Caribbean Planning for Adaptation to Climate Change (CPACC) Project." http://www.caricom.org /jsp/projects/macc percent20project/cpacc.jsp.

29. Caribbean Community Secretariat. "Adaptation to Climate Change in the Caribbean (ACCC) Project." http://www.caricom.org/jsp /projects/macc percent20project/accc.jsp.

30. Image Source: Mary Veira/IPS.

31. Center for Responsible Travel. Innovators Think Tank: Climate Change and Coastal & Marine Tourism, July 22 – 24, 2015. http:// innovators2015.com/.

32. Andrew Burger. (December 1, 2014). "Renewable Energy: `Development as Freedom' in Haiti and Beyond." *Triple Pundit*. http:// www.triplepundit.com/2014/12/renewable-energy-development -freedom-haiti-beyond/.

33. Anastasia Pantsios. (July 9, 2015). "Belize Joins Ten Island Challenge to Transition to 100% Renewable Energy." *EcoWatch.* http://ecowatch.com/2015/07/09/belize-ten-island-challenge/.

34. Carrie Thompson. (2013). "How Aruba Plans to Be Energy Independent by 2020." *Sustainable Brands.* http://www.sustainable brands.com/news_and_views/clean_tech/carrie-thompson/how -aruba-plans-be-energy-independent-2020.

35. Kaitlyn Bunker. (2015). "A Caribbean Island Says Goodbye Diesel and Hello 100 percent Renewable Energy." *GreenBiz.* http://blog.rmi.org /blog_2015_01_07_a_caribbean_island_says_goodbye_to_diesel _fuel.

36. Robert Youngs. (2015). "Will the Caribbean Become the Next Hotbed for Renewable Energy?" http://www.greenbiz.com/article /will-caribbean-become-next-hotbed-renewable-energy.

37. Van Hilderbrand and Josh Sturtevant. (July 21, 2015). "The Stage is Set in Cuba for a Boom in Renewable Energy Investment; Can U.S. Companies Take Advantage?" *Energy Finance Report.* http:// www.energyfinancereport.com/2015/07/the-stage-is-set-in-cuba -for-a-boom-in-renewable-energy-investment-can-u-s-companies -take-advantage/.

Case Study 4.1

Disconnect between Timelines and Investments by Resort Owners and Operators

by Andrea Pinabell

Coastal hotels and resorts face a unique set of circumstances in balancing guest expectations and minimizing operational costs in the wake of new weather patterns, including those due to climate change. Within the Caribbean's coastal zones, climate change related issues span from the changing length of seasonal patterns to more frequent/severe hurricanes and other storms. Operating successful hotels and resorts takes balancing a dedicated staff with the passion to deliver an excellent guest experience, an inviting and attractive property, and efficient operating systems. With utility costs being the second highest operating cost for most properties, it is imperative for owners and operators to minimize costs without diminishing that guest experience. It is this balance that will determine the profitability of the property and its long-term success.

What Are the Two Primary Ways to Enhance the Incremental Value of a Hotel or Resort?

There are two primary ways to enhance the incremental value of a hotel or resort (Fig. 4.1).

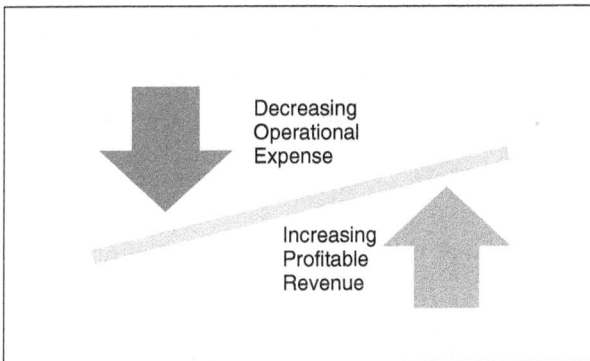

Decreasing
Operational
Expense

Increasing
Profitable
Revenue

Figure 4.1 Impact of Reducing Utility Cost on Asset Value[1]

The first is by decreasing the utility costs incurred by the property. This would include costs such as energy (electricity, natural gas, and district heating and cooling), water (both chilled water and municipal water and sewer), and waste (landfilled and recycled). By decreasing these operational expenses, an owner can increase the GOPAR, or gross operating profit per available room, that the resort achieves.

The second way to positively impact a property's incremental value is through increasing its profitable revenue. This type of asset growth is typically achieved through increased bookings and therefore higher occupancies. Over the property's life span, both of these ways to increase incremental value require capital outlay by the owner.

What Is the Difference between Operating Expense and Capital Expense?

The main expenses that an owner incurs in the operation of a hotel or resort fall into two main categories: Operating Expenses and Capital Expenses (CapEx). Operating expenses include utility costs, expenses for consumables such as light bulbs, foodstuffs, and paper, and project costs (including replacement fixtures) that have a return on investment (ROI) of less than 12 months. Capital expenses are larger investments to the property and include projects like new brand programming, hotel or property renovations, and physical plant or building upgrades.

Herein lies the push–pull scenario that all owners, including Starwood owners and operators, have with regard to maintaining and increasing the value of their asset. Starwood[2] has 1,300-plus properties in over 100 countries worldwide, including 16 in the Caribbean. In 2016, Starwood became the first U.S.-headquartered hotel company in nearly 60 years to own/manage a hotel in Cuba, with several additional properties in the pipeline.

How Do Owners Decide Where to Invest Capital in Their Properties?

Every owner has to ask him/herself a few questions in order to determine where is the best place to spend their capital in order to get the highest

ROI. For most owners, their ROI threshold is approximately 3 years. In addition, it has been widely accepted that investment in *guest facing* parts of the property will drive top-line revenue and therefore, is a safe investment option for owners (Table 4.2).

Table 4.2: Investment Scenarios[3]

Guest Facing	Back of House
Rooms renovation	Upgraded boiler or chiller
Lobby renovation	Combined heat and power system
High efficiency lighting retrofit	Building Energy Management system
Updated pool decking	Liquid pool covers
Brand programming	Installation of solar

Investment in *back of house,* or the property's utility systems, drives energy and water efficiency, thermal consistency for guest and meeting rooms, and lower utility costs. Even though energy and water costs are rising and thermal consistency aids in overall guest satisfaction, the ROI for these types of systems and facility upgrades have an ROI of 5 to 10 years, which is greater than the average owner threshold of 3 years. Herein lies the disconnect between the time frame or ROI threshold for owners and the capital required for investment in *back of house* or efficiency driving projects.

What Are Some Possible Solutions for Overcoming This Disconnect?

At Starwood, we have worked to overcome this disconnect through a variety of ways:

1. Environmental goals
2. Foundational Initiatives
3. Innovative financing and vendor partnerships.

The first is through environmental goals. Having a rallying cry that our properties can get behind has been crucial for us to drive efficiency. Our "30/20 by 2020" campaign is Starwood's commitment to reduce our energy use and GHG emissions by 30 percent and our water consumption by 20 percent by the year 2020. These goals may be simple in form but frame a multifaceted strategy including many of the required and recommended initiatives and programs that Starwood has, including guest-facing programs like *Make a Green Choice*.[4]

The second is through what we call Foundational Initiatives. These are low- to no-cost operational and project changes that have an ROI of about one year. These projects include high-efficiency lighting, low flow faucets and fixtures, and smart irrigation systems, in addition to operational changes like temperature set points and closing of sheer curtains within the guest rooms. This is important because the owner can utilize operating capital and not have to go through the CapEx planning process. In addition, with an ROI within a typical owner's threshold, we can start to build a commitment for sustainability through increased profitability.

Finally, innovative financing has become increasingly important. Throughout our portfolio, the Foundational Initiatives have been substantially completed. The projects that remain from the third party energy and water audits that were completed at each property are the more expensive projects that have an ROI that is typically greater than the owner's 3 year threshold. In order to circumvent this issue to get these efficiency projects completed, innovative financing was introduced. Innovative financing includes nontraditional vendor contracts such as Power Purchase Agreements (PPA), which is a mechanism for purchasing power directly from the vendor, Lease Agreements in which one leases the equipment from the vendor, and financing through utility bill savings, which is typical if financed through one's local power company. Other innovative financing mechanisms have also been piloted and explored such as Managed Energy Services Agreements (MESA)[i] and private equity funding.

In conclusion, a disconnect does exist between relevant return expectations and efficiency-driven projects, but we believe that through a strategic and creative approach, this gap can be bridged.

---

[i] A Managed Energy Service Agreement (MESA) is broader than an Energy Service Agreement (ESA) because the provider also assumes the broader energy management of a client's facility, including the responsibility for utility bills, in exchange for a series of payments based on the customer's historic energy use. MESAs offer promise for energy retrofits when the hotel or other retail business is financially stable, but lacks the expertise or time to undertake the energy efficiency retrofit.

Notes

1. Figure Source: Andrea Pinabell

2. Starwood Hotels & Resorts. www.starwoodhotels.com.

3. Table Source: Andrea Pinabell

4. Starwood Hotels & Resorts. "Global Citizenship Sustainability Programs & Initiatives: Make a Green Choice" http://www.starwoodhotels .com/corporate/about/citizenship/sustainability/programs.html? language=en_US.

Case Study 4.2

Bucuti & Tara Beach Resort, Aruba: The Evolution of a Deep Green Resort

by Amy Kerr and Tisa LaSorte

As Earth's vital signs continue declining at an alarming rate, hotelier and noted environmentalist Ewald Biemans, founder of Bucuti & Tara Beach Resort,[1] a 104-room property in Aruba, knew more than 20 years ago it could no longer be business as usual. Rising sea levels, hotter surface temperatures, warming oceans, and shrinking ice sheets captured Biemans' attention, prompting him to take the first step toward a safer future.[2] One step became two, and eventually compounded, so that today Bucuti & Tara Beach Resort thrives at the forefront of sustainable tourism.[3]

Located on Eagle Beach among Aruba's low-rise resorts, Bucuti & Tara Beach Resort is recognized by TripAdvisor as the Best Hotel in the Caribbean.[4] The resort also holds more eco-certifications of any Caribbean property, and is a pioneer in demonstrating that guests can enjoy vacations of a lifetime with minimal impact on the environment. In October 2016, Bucuti & Tara was named the "Most Sustainable Hotel & Resort in the World" by the international certifying body Green Globe, scoring 98 out of 100 on Green Globe's sustainability criteria.[5] Bucuti's meaning of sustainability is significantly broader and deeper than siloed green initiatives; it is an intrinsic way of life. *Green* is an all-encompassing commitment to renewable resources, preserving nature, being environmentally conscious, sourcing locally and ethically, celebrating native culture, and being an active member of the greater community.[6]

Turning the First Green Step into a Way of Life

Bucuti's story began in the 1980s when Biemans noticed an increase in pollution and problems created by Aruba's growing tourism industry. As a nature lover, Biemans was dismayed at the drastic increase of hotel construction damaging Aruba's delicate ecosystem and the increasing quantities of waste appear on beaches and roadsides. In his words, the final wake-up call was a German guest at Bucuti scoffing at a beer served in a disposable plastic mug whereas Europeans had already begun the practice of reducing, reusing, and recycling. It was that moment when Biemans decided to eliminate unnecessary plastic and implement additional environmental safeguards.

As a tiny island devoid of natural resources and export potential, Aruba was and continues to be heavily dependent upon tourism. Looking ahead, Biemans saw a bleak future where financial survival depended on high occupancy, yet rapidly rising sea levels on already sea level-based Aruba threatened the survival of coastal tourism as well as the island's greater environment.[7] Biemans began researching and installing as many measures as possible to reduce GHG emissions and energy consumption so that Bucuti could begin lessening its carbon footprint.[8]

Over more than two decades, Bucuti has carefully built upon its earliest initiatives. Today, Bucuti leads as a successful green resort that generates and meets the needs of a large volume of guests while being a good steward of the environment. Seeing the bigger picture, the resort openly shares its best practices and encourages others to do the same.

Biemans has found that green certified standards are valuable tools to measure and improve environmental impacts. Bucuti, which was the first resort to receive International Organization for Standardization (ISO) 14001[9] in the Americas, is Green Globe[10] and Travelife[11] certified, and is the only LEED® Silver certified[12] property in the Caribbean. Each certification varies in focus and depth, but all require tracking, which is imperative to developing environmentally friendly habits, establishing benchmarks, and achieving realistic expectations. The certifications promote consistent best practices and guide properties on their journey to make a difference[13] (Case Study 4.4).

Being Green Saves More than the Environment

In the hotel business, there are two ways to thrive. One is to increase rates, which leads to customer dissatisfaction, and the second is to reduce energy and water consumption drastically and pass along the savings. Bucuti actively chooses to do the latter. Contrary to the belief that being green is cost-prohibitive, Bucuti's energy conservation measures have reduced

Image 4.2.1 Bucuti's Ewald Biemans proudly showcases certification recognitions and guest satisfaction awards side by side, highlighting that hotels can be successful and sustainable.[14]

operating costs and allowed the resort to pass along some savings to its guests by maintaining reasonable rates.

Bucuti believes that achieving green success can only happen when everyone—staff, guests, and vendors—shares in the plan. Bucuti's approach is two-fold: communicate what and why green initiatives are implemented *and* ensure actions match pledged policies. Bucuti's certifications and sustainability manager works with all staff and vendors to implement practical and measurable solutions. Guests can learn about the initiatives and how they can participate through a variety of ongoing messaging from their private concierge during in-room check-in, through the resort's environmental television channel, on Bucuti's website and social media, to signage and collateral throughout the resort. Guests can participate in reducing their carbon footprint through, for instance, the Green Stay Program, reusable canteens, and in-room climate control.

Image 4.2.2 After learning about Bucuti's Green Stay program, guests can indicate their participation by putting this card on the room door.[15]

A Cohesive Approach

Bucuti's holistic approach to sustainability includes five key areas: design and construction, water efficiency, energy efficiency, materials and resources, and indoor environmental quality. Each of these considers the health and safety of guests, staff, and the environment within the resort and beyond.[16]

Design and construction

In the competitive world of coastal resorts, there is great pressure to gain occupancy revenue and recognition by falling into the trap of bigger and newer. Bucuti proves that guests can have an excellent, top-ranking experience by not overbuilding, not overusing, and not abusing its facilities and its natural environment.

Investing in sustainable construction and design is key to this preservation. In 2013–2015, the resort underwent a retrofitting process to achieve LEED Silver certification, which entailed implementing sustainable design measures wherever possible throughout the resort. The Tara Wing, for instance, includes blocks made from recycled material and doors and molding made from farmed wood. Windows are insulated and reflective. The fitness center flooring is made of recycled tires. The furniture in the lobby is created from recycled plastic material.

Water efficiency

Aruba's extremely arid climate coupled with no freshwater source makes the island dependent on seawater desalination to meet all its potable water requirements. Because of the high cost of desalination, this process cannot reasonably meet the resort's entire water demand.[17]

Bucuti has therefore sought methods to reduce its water consumption while minimizing impact on the environment. Between 2005 and 2016, the resort reduced water usage by 37 percent, even as annual occupancy averaged more than 90 percent. All water fixtures have aerators and rooms and public showers have low-flow showerheads leading to savings on both water and energy.[18] Multiple measures have contributed to this success. Gray water[i] collected from the laundry, dining facilities, guest rooms, and public restrooms along with rainwater collected from rooftops are used for the resort's irrigation. Washing machines are loaded to full capacity to maximize each cycle. Only water-efficient equipment is procured including HACCP-approved[ii] faucets, toilets, and shower heads, which reduces flow by 60 percent. Recently, Bucuti pledged to be part of the Water

---

[i] Gray water is gently used water from sinks, showers, tubs, and washing machines. It does not include water that has come into contact with any potentially biologically harmful substances.

[ii] HACCP stands for Hazard Analysis and Critical Control Points. HACCP is a management system in which food safety is addressed through the analysis and control of biological, chemical, and physical hazards from raw material production, procurement and handling, to manufacturing, distribution and consumption of the finished product."Hazard Analysis Critical Control Point (HACCP)." U.S. Food and Drug Administration. Hazard Analysis Critical Control Point (HACCP).

Sense H$_2$0tel Challenge, a U.S. Environmental Protection Agency (EPA) initiative to track usage performance measures and reduce consumption. Bucuti is the only resort outside North America currently participating.

Bucuti also invites guests to participate in its Green Stay Program through which they elect to reduce housekeeping services to twice weekly. In addition to conserving water, energy, and cleaning supplies, it also reduces labor. Bed linens are changed only on Wednesday and Saturday (or on request and at check out), and towels are only changed if found on the floor or upon request. In-room signage encourages guests to join the effort by showing them how they can help save water.

The resort maximizes its use of gray water, and LEED requires at least 50 percent of water usage/consumption (grounds, landscaping) is gray or recaptured water. A three-chamber water tank holds gray water from laundry, restaurant, and guest rooms for use in irrigation. Sprinklers are on timers that adjust depending on the amount of rainfall and are only active for up to three minutes per day.

Energy efficiency

Bucuti takes a strategic approach to its efforts to mitigate climate change by seeking solutions for both long-term benefits and immediate impact. The resort conducted an assessment to identify its number one consumption of energy and tackled it head-on. After discovering that air-conditioning alone comprised 60 percent of total energy cost, the resort promptly installed Variable Refrigerant Flow (VRF) A/C units, an energy-saving technology that allows for changes in temperature in different parts of a building at various times of day.[19]

The resort also installed the INNCOM energy management system, ecoMODE, through which Bucuti guests opt-in to the resort's sustainability program with the press of a "Green Button" on their thermostat. The button triggers an enhanced energy savings setback, which automatically increases in-room temperatures when unoccupied and resets to the guest's preference upon reentry. When used to its fullest potential, the system reduces energy costs by 20 to 30 percent.[20]

As energy-efficient technology becomes more advanced, Bucuti is swift to adopt and implement new equipment. Having once used compact fluorescent

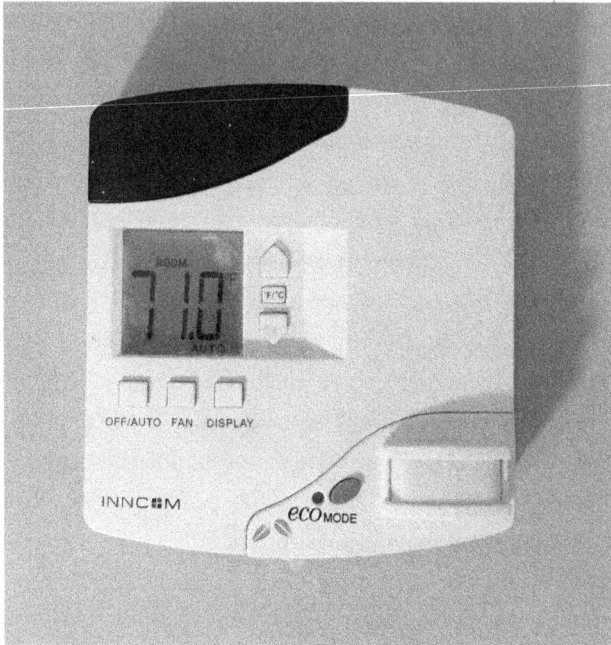

Image 4.2.3 The ecoMODE setting on the thermostat allows for automated temperature controls based upon room occupancy.[21]

lighting (CFL), the resort has now switched to light emitting diode (LED) light bulbs. While the upfront cost is higher for LED light bulbs, the long-term benefits and cost-savings are much greater because they use less power and have a longer life span than CFL light bulbs. In addition, all lights work on timers or motion sensors to further reduce GHG emissions. Bucuti has one of the lowest per-occupied-room electricity usage of all hotels in Aruba.

To further reduce GHG emissions, Bucuti either purchases ENERGY STAR rated appliances or actively seeks out alternative energy-efficient appliances.[22] The property's 16 thermal solar panels, which can each heat up to 100 gallons of water per day, heat all water used throughout the resort. Bucuti also derives 20 percent of its electricity through the island's wind turbines.

Material and resources

Bucuti is committed to reducing, reusing, and recycling resources in order to decrease energy expenditure. In an effort to reduce its carbon footprint, the resort sources local supplies and products made on-island whenever possible, purchases cleaning supplies and toiletries in bulk, converts damaged linens and bath towels to pillowcases and hand towels, and uses bio-degradable and eco-friendly products, including cleaning detergents and marketing materials. Additionally, the resort requires its vendor partners to use environmentally certified products and adhere to environmental best practices. By identifying such areas of opportunity within day-to-day operations, however small they may seem individually, Bucuti has made significant strides in protecting the environment.

The resort has an extensive recycling system with separate bins throughout the property for glass, aluminum, and paper and cardboard. Back-of-house recycling bins also collect green glass, batteries, and vegetable oil. According to Bucuti's bi-annual audits, the resort recycles and reuses on average 60 to 70 percent of guests' disposed trash.

Currently, the island of Aruba does not recycle plastic, and plastic waste goes to the island's landfill. Bucuti has therefore actively sought to reduce use of plastics. Upon arrival, each guest receives a reusable water bottle to eliminate the impacts caused by disposable plastic bottles. In more than six years since the program began, it is estimated that Bucuti has kept nearly two million plastic bottles out of Aruba's landfill.

Bucuti also hosts a monthly beach clean-up and invites guests and staff to participate. The 20-year-old program removes on average 500 lbs. of waste from the beach each year, helping to reduce emissions and protect Aruba's natural resources and marine life, including nesting endangered leatherback turtles.[23]

Indoor environmental quality

Bucuti's goal is to provide guests with an eco-room that is both safe, healthy, and irritant-free while minimizing energy consumption. Because of Aruba's location near the equator, high humidity and moisture levels can cause mold and mildew.

While chlorofluorocarbons (CFCs) and gas-operated air conditioners dehumidify ambient air, they also release hazardous gases into the atmosphere. To prevent such toxins, Bucuti's energy-efficient air-conditioning system utilizes water to cool the air. The resort combats allergens, mold, and mildew through the use of HEPA (High Efficiency Particulate Air) air purifiers and dehumidifiers, both of which are less harmful to the environment than the alternative.[24] In addition, all of the rooms at Bucuti are nonsmoking, abiding by the LEED certification requirement to prohibit smoking within 25 feet of a building.[25]

Next Steps for a Safer Future

Bucuti carefully plans its introduction of new green initiatives. Next steps include implementing a Smart Metering online utility tracking system,[26] double-up laundry water recycling set to save 400,000 gallons of water each year,[27] and the installation of additional photovoltaic solar panels to further reduce electricity dependency.[28]

Bucuti's journey toward a greener, safer resort has entailed deviating from accustomed, widely accepted business practices, and has required time and resources to research and implement new options. Building one green initiative upon another has created a path toward a more successful way to do business. Along the way, Bucuti has been able to prove that a rewarding vacation and sustainable tourism can be mutually *inclusive*.

Notes

1. Bucuti & Tara Beach Resort. "Eco Friendly." https://www.bucuti .com/eco-friendly

2. One of the many articles about Ewald Biemans is by Alexander Britell. (April 18, 2013). "Making Caribbean Hotels Sustainable: An Interview With Aruba's Ewald Biemans." *Caribbean Journal.* http:// www.caribjournal.com/2013/04/18/making-caribbean-hotels -sustainable-an-interview-with-arubas-ewald-biemans/#.

3. Center for Responsible Travel. (2016). "Caribbean Green Travel: Your Choices Make a Difference." http://www.responsibletravel .org/news/films.html. This documentary film contains a segment on Bucuti & Tara's sustainability practices.

4. TripAdvisor. (2015). "2015 Top 25 Hotels - Caribbean." http:// www.tripadvisor.com/TravelersChoice-Hotels-cTop-g147237.

5. Green Globe. (October 18, 2016). "Bucuti & Tara Beach Resort Aruba Certified Most Sustainable Hotel & Resort in the World." http://greenglobe.com/latest-news/bucuti-tara-beach-resort-aruba -certified-most-sustainable-hotel-resort-in-the-world/

6. Bucuti & Tara Beach Resort. "Eco Friendly: What We Do." https:// www.bucuti.com/eco-friendly#what-we-do.

7. NASA's Jet Propulsion Laboratory. (October 21, 2015).

8. Ewald Biemans. (October 15, 2013). "Our Little World Called Aruba." http://www.bucuti.com/blog/ewald-k-biemans/our-little-world -called-aruba.

9. International Organization for Standardization. (2015). "ISO 14000 - Environmental Management." http://www.iso.org/iso/iso_catalogue /management_standards/iso_9000_iso_14000/iso14000.

10. Green Globe. (2015). http://greenglobe.com/.

11. TraveLife. (2015). http://travelifecollection.com/home.

12. U.S. Green Building Council. (2015). http://www.usgbc.org/projects /bucuti-and-tara-beach-resorts.

13. Ewald Biemans. (February 22, 2013). " What It Means to be Green." http://www.bucuti.com/blog/ewald-k-biemans/what-it-means -be-green.

14. Image Source: Bucuti & Tara Beach Resort.

15. Image Source: Bucuti & Tara Beach Resort.

16. Ewald Biemans. (April 7, 2010). "Bucuti & Tara Beach Resorts: Environmental Practices & Energy Conservation." http://www.bucuti .com/sites/default/files/pdf/D52_Environmental_Practices10.pdf.

17. AquaTech. (2015). "Aruba Promises the Best Water in the Caribbean." http://www.aquatech.com/project-profiles/aruba-promises-best -water-caribbean/.

18. Earth Easy. (2015). "Low-Flow Aerators/Showerheads." http:// eartheasy.com/live_lowflow_aerators.htm.

19. Perfect Infraengineers Ltd. (n.d.). "VRV and VRF Air Conditioning Systems." http://www.vrvairconditioner.com/.

20. INNCOM by Honeywell. (2015). "Explore the Solutions." http:// www.inncom.com/.

21. Image Source: Bucuti & Tara Beach Resort.

22. United States Enivronmental Protection Agency. (2015). "How a Product Earns the ENERGY STAR Label." http://www.energystar. gov/products/how-product-earns-energy-star-label.

23. 15 ATV. (April 27, 2015). *15on15 - Bucuti & Tara Beach Resorts - Beach Clean Up.* Video. Eagle Beach, Aruba, Dutch Caribbean. https://www.youtube.com/watch?v=n1WoGDiBAxc.

24. Ewald Biemans. (March 16, 2013). "Let's Clear the Air." http:// www.bucuti.com/blog/ewald-k-biemans/let's-clear-air.

25. U.S. Green Building Council. (2015). "Environmental Tobacco Smoke Control." http://www.usgbc.org/credits/healthcare/v4-draft /eqp2.

26. Smart Grid. (2015). "Smart Meters." http://www.whatissmartgrid .org/smart-grid-101/smart-meters?gclid=CJWWt7jV-80CFVFcfgo dTzAJGg.

27. Ozone Water Technologies. (2015). http://ozonewatertech.com/.

28. Solar Energy Industries Association. (2015). "Photovoltaic (Solar Electric)." http://www.seia.org/policy/solar-technology/photovoltaic -solar-electric.

Case Study 4.3
Grupo Puntacana: The Keys to Sustainable Tourism

by Jake Kheel

In 1969, a group of adventurous investors, led by labor lawyer Theodore W. Kheel, bought a large parcel of uninhabited land in Punta Cana on the eastern shore of the Dominican Republic. They had no idea what use they might make of the land. They partnered with a young Dominican, Frank Rainieri, who convinced them that in spite of the previous decades of the brutal Trujillo dictatorship, the subsequent occupation of the island by the United States after his assassination, and a total lack of public infrastructure in Punta Cana, the future of their property and the Dominican Republic, was in tourism. Together, the American investors and Rainieri took a seemingly ill-advised bet on tourism and created a company, Grupo Puntacana (GPC).[i] Limited by a lack of money, but blessed with great creativity and a deep respect for the people and natural environment of the Dominican Republic, GPC was forced to adapt to its circumstances, providing many important lessons that can inform sustainable tourism even today.

During the ensuing 45 years, this unique partnership grew Grupo Puntacana into one of the most successful companies in the Dominican Republic. Grupo Puntacana, which comprises the largest international airport in the country, luxury hotel properties, an expansive golf resort community, and a privately held electric and water utility, became the catalyst that started large-scale tourism growth in the Dominican Republic.

Today Punta Cana has over 38,000 hotel rooms, more than half the 60,000 rooms in the Dominican Republic as a whole. And the Dominican Republic has become the Caribbean's top tourism destination.[1] Dominican tourism provides tens of thousands of jobs, hundreds of millions of dollars in foreign investment, and significant economic opportunity in diverse segments of the economy beyond tourism.

---

[i] Punta Cana is the geographical location, while Puntacana is the business name.

However, the history of Grupo Puntacana is exceptional not simply because of its economic success and its impact on the development of the Dominican Republic. GPC's deep commitment to environmental protection and community development, long before the term *sustainable development* had even been invented, was one of its most significant contributions to Dominican tourism.[2]

Alongside the development of resorts and tourism infrastructure, GPC also undertook a range of social and environmental projects that grew into two permanent institutions, The Puntacana Foundation dedicated to improving the social and economic welfare of local communities and the Puntacana Ecological Foundation dedicated to research and projects to protect and improve the environment. (In 2016, the two foundations merged into one institution, the Grupo Puntacana Foundation, combining both missions.[ii]) From the outset, Grupo Puntacana viewed these projects not as charities but as mutually beneficial investments that strengthened the business and community while protecting the environment. And these two Foundations also have become important tools for helping to address some of the impacts of climate change on Puntacana and elsewhere in the Caribbean.

Social Sustainability: Build a Community, Not a Resort

A key ingredient to starting and operating any hotel or resort project is hiring qualified employees. Yet in the early years, Punta Cana not only lacked qualified staff, but there also wasn't a local population big enough to hire from and train as workers. Grupo Puntacana, the first new business in the region, would somehow have to create its own workforce.

The First School

One of the companies' earliest undertakings was to build and staff a small school on the property. The school, which provided a modest, but

---

[ii] As of January 2016, the Puntacana Ecological Foundation and the Puntacana Foundation merged to become the Grupo Puntacana Foundation. Within this essay, the references to the two separate organizations remain since we are primarily describing the period before the merger.

previously unavailable, education for the local children, was by no means a purely charitable endeavor. The distances and poor roads made daily travel to Punta Cana from the isolated communities in the area impossible. Not to mention that GPC didn't have the money or vehicles to provide transportation.

In fact, building a school would provide multiple services that benefitted both the local people and the business. The school attracted families, previously dispersed throughout the region, to live and work closer to the Grupo Puntacana property, creating a potential labor force that did not previously exist. It provided a basic education to the local children and improved their chances for progress and potentially as future employees. Similarly, these early families became loyal to the company and committed to the region. As much a strategy of corporate social responsibility (CSR), the school was also an early example of human resource development.

Puntacana Village

This mutually beneficial strategy of combining CSR and human resource development proved to be so successful that Grupo Puntacana would employ it again later on. In the early 1990s, Grupo Puntacana began a modest residential community called Puntacana Village. It was initially designed as a simple cluster of homes for GPC employees. However, GPC quickly realized that this small development could be an important tool for attracting qualified professionals from Santo Domingo and elsewhere in the island. Puntacana Village included a bilingual school, a church, and a park in its early design, and this created a safe and healthy environment for families who began to move to Punta Cana permanently.

Puntacana Village has since become a bustling community with hundreds of private homes and condos and dozens of private businesses. Importantly, it has enticed a significant number of professionals and entrepreneurs to the region, improving the quality of the local talent pool and the overall competitiveness of the destination. The Puntacana International School now has over 500 students and competes with some of the best schools in the country. What seemed to be a simple contribution to local education has become a key strategy for building the competitiveness of the region.

Ann and Ted Kheel Polytechnic School

This strategy was also applied in the local community, outside of the hotels and resorts of the region. In 1998, GPC created the not-for-profit charity, The Puntacana Foundation, to promote sustainable economic growth through focusing on education and health in the local communities in and around Punta Cana, particularly in the nearby community of Veron. The town of Veron is made up of tens of thousands of Dominicans and Haitians, mostly unskilled laborers who have migrated to Punta Cana from all over the island in search of employment. Veron has thousands of rudimentary houses and businesses built on a linear path along the original road to Higuey.

However, Veron has received almost no public investment in infrastructure such as schools, hospitals, or sewer system, because, in an ironic twist, the millions of tourists visiting Punta Cana, who provide tens of millions of dollars of annual tax revenue to the central government, are not able to vote in favor of the region. Migrants who arrive from other parts of the island generally vote in their hometowns. As a result, nearly all public services including electricity, water distribution, sewage treatment, road infrastructure, and schools are paid for by the private sector. Made up almost entirely of migrants from other parts of the island, this peri-urban landscape has scattered neighborhoods and improvised shantytowns but little collective history or sense of community.

In 2003, Grupo Puntacana built the Ann and Ted Kheel Polytechnic School to provide public high school education to the children of Veron. It was, at the time, the only public high school within 50 square miles of the international airport. In addition to basic high school, the Polytechnic also offered technical training in electricity, plumbing, restaurant service, and English language.

This was not simply a charitable endeavor to help the children of Veron. The Polytechnic School was strategically designed to teach skills and trades directly needed in the tourism sector, providing jobs for graduating students and giving them better quality of work in the industry. Importantly, the school encourages individuals to establish roots in the region and start families, creating a more permanent, less migratory populace, which has started to give the town a sense of place. While Veron is still rife with social problems, the Polytechnic School is one of the few well-established institutions benefiting the people of Veron.

Image 4.3.1 The Ann and Ted Kheel Polytechnic School[3]

Environmental Sustainability: Creation through Innovation

Early on, Grupo Puntacana also began addressing a range of environmental problems. It recognized that the success of tourism in the region, including the hotels, residential properties, golf courses, and airport, all depended on protecting a healthy land and marine environment.

Puntacana Ecological Foundation: A think tank for innovation

In 1994, Grupo Puntacana formed the not-for-profit Puntacana Ecological Foundation to develop a range of experimental projects that confront different environmental challenges. Grupo Puntacana realized that if its own hotels and the dozens of other hotels in the region are to continue to be successful in the future, they must protect the local environment. The Ecological Foundation, rather than a charity that makes a smattering of donations to different causes, was created to implement living, breathing solutions to environmental threats in order to make the tourism industry more environmentally sustainable. The Foundation uses the Grupo Puntacana property as a laboratory to implement projects and then shares those experiences with other businesses, universities, and governments, all with the aim of making the tourism industry more sustainable in the long term. It has grown from a Foundation supported initially by Grupo Puntacana into an active collaborator that attracts funding from national and international foundations, multilateral organizations, companies, and revenue-generating projects and partnerships. Several projects provide examples of the unique role the Foundation is playing as a sustainable tourism think tank.

The Center for Sustainability

Built in 2001, the Center for Sustainability engages some of the best universities in the world in research and education programs in an effort to provide solutions to some of the tourism industry's greatest social and environmental challenges. The Ecological Foundation has engaged Harvard, Cornell, and Virginia Tech, among other universities to research diverse subjects related to sustainability in the Punta Cana region.

For example, since 2008, the Ecological Foundation has conducted water quality studies jointly with Virginia Tech. This work made apparent that the contamination from untreated sewage in the community of Veron was affecting the health of the local people as well as posing a threat to the local freshwater aquifers that also serve the tourism industry. Based on these studies, the Foundation created the Fuentes de Vida community project. It assembled a group of project partners to design and construct a community-scale water treatment facility in the neighborhood

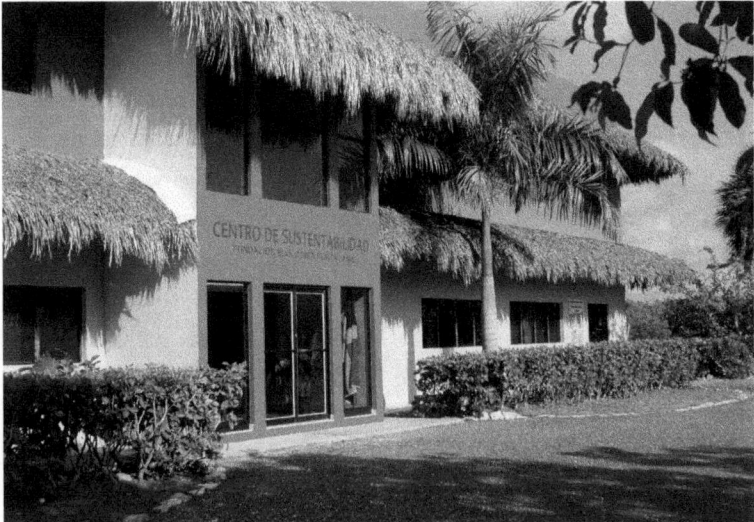

Image 4.3.2 The Center for Sustainability at Puntacana Resort & Club[4]

of Domingo Maiz. The group determined that a *constructed wetland* was an appropriate technology that could be scaled for different communities and effectively filter sewage using plants and microorganisms to treat human waste. The partners fundraised for close to three years, and the system was inaugurated in 2014.

The constructed wetland currently treats the waste of over 150 families in Dominico Maiz. Continued water quality monitoring has demonstrated that the system is successfully filtering the community's sewage, improving community health, and reducing the risk to the aquifer. This project could be replicated in Veron, as a solution to its sewage problems.

Zero Waste

In 2007, the Ecological Foundation designed and implemented one of the largest integrated solid waste projects in the Dominican Republic, a large, well-managed Recycling Center that today recycles or composts over 55 percent of the waste generated by Grupo Puntacana. This, in turn, contributes significantly to avoided carbon production. A local auditor estimates that GPC's recycling efforts save over 405,000 kilowatt hours of energy consumption and over 130,000 gallons of water in a month. The Center is also a hub for promoting the value of integrated waste management, receiving dozens of monthly visits from local schools, businesses, and even government agencies; it has also been turned into a case study by the Barna Business School in Santo Domingo.

GPC's Zero Waste project was the first of its kind in the Dominican Republic. In Punta Cana, the volume of recyclable material produced by GPC helped create a market for recyclable materials in the Punta Cana region, facilitating purchasers of recyclable materials to move into the region in search of materials. This market has encouraged dozens of hotels and resorts to begin recycling programs within their properties, rather than pay to landfill the materials.

Confronting climate change

Many of the Ecological Foundation's programs directly or indirectly relate to GPC's growing concerns about climate change. As a coastal community

Image 4.3.3 Since 2014, the Puntacana Ecological Foundation's Staghorn coral restoration program has returned over 2.7 km of nursery-reared tissue to natural reefs.[5]

that confronts many challenges, climate change has the potential to bring about rapid and new challenges that represent threats to the tourism industry. The Ecological Foundation's coral restoration work (discussed in Volume 1 Marine Tourism, Case Study 2.1) responds to the loss of critical coral species to disease and attempts to cultivate remaining coral genotypes that have proven resilient to variable water temperature and disease. Similarly, the Ecological Foundation has engaged its university partners at the Harvard Graduate School of Design and Syracuse University to engage students in planning and design projects that create resilient coastal communities, adapted to real-world challenges such as climate change.

Conclusions

The tourism industry is different from nearly all other modern industries. Most industries manufacture a product or service that is not necessarily specific to a place or community. In tourism, the product *is* the place. The product *is* the community. Tourism sells natural, cultural, and human resources the same way that a factory sells a car or a piece of furniture. When these resources are protected and allowed to prosper, tourism flourishes. Sadly, there is no shortage of examples of tourism destinations that have failed due to poor environmental protection.

Grupo Puntacana exemplifies the complex nature of sustainable development. It is an unapologetic for-profit entity that is developing the eastern coast of the Dominican Republic in order to lure foreign and domestic visitors and investment. Its capacity to attract visitors comes from a combination of natural and human resources, so it serves its own financial best interest both to preserve the local environment of the island and to provide opportunities for advancement for the local populace.

In its origin, in its current imaging, and in its future growth, Grupo Puntacana embodies the notion that sustainable development means community education and progress, environmental management, and innovation in the face of enormous limitations and challenges. Today climate change represents the latest in a long line of challenges that Grupo Puntacana is seeking to address through its social and environmental programs. Grupo Puntacana's recognition, from its origins, that tourism's economic success is dependent on its local natural and human resources is rare and noteworthy.

Notes

1. Gay Nagle Myers. (May 21, 2014). "Dominican Republic Tops in Caribbean Tourism, and Growing." *Travel Weekly.* http://www .travelweekly.com/Caribbean-Travel/Dominican-Republic-tops -in-Caribbean-tourism-and-growing/.
2. Center for Responsible Travel. (2016). "Caribbean Green Travel: Your Choices Make a Difference." http://www.responsibletravel.org /news/films.html. This documentary film includes several segments on Puntacana's sustainable tourism practices.
3. Image Source: Grupo Puntacana Foundation.
4. Image Source: Grupo Puntacana Foundation.
5. Image Source: Grupo Puntacana Foundation.

Case Study 4.4:

Caribbean Hotel Energy Efficiency and Renewable Energy Action (CHENACT)

by Loreto Duffy-Mayers

During the global economic crisis between 2008 and 2011, the Caribbean tourism sector experienced a series of challenges, including declining visitors and visitor spending, increasing global competition, and increasing input costs, particularly for energy. In response, the Caribbean Hotel Energy Efficiency and Renewable Energy Action (CHENACT) was launched in 2012 with funding from four international organizations and the government of Barbados.[1] Its mission has been to improve energy efficiency, reduce utility costs, and mitigate GHG emissions in the Caribbean hotel sector. Three regional organizations, the Caribbean Hotel and Tourism Association (CHTA), the Caribbean Alliance for Sustainable Tourism (CAST), and the Caribbean Tourism Organization (CTO), which collectively represent the interests of the hotel sector and tourism industry, were tasked with implementing the CHENACT program. Overall, CHENACT hopes to benefit the entire tourism industry by:

- Making energy usage more efficient in the Caribbean hotel sector;
- Reducing energy costs to hotels;
- Increasing competitiveness in the hotel sector through lower operating costs;
- Increasing the use of renewable energies;
- Generating positive environmental impacts such as reduction of greenhouse gases and ozone depleting substances;
- Generating a positive environmental footprint and attracting more environmentally aware consumers and industry players such as tour operators and airlines; and
- Generating additional revenue from the sale of carbon emission reductions/carbon credits.[i]

---

[i] Carbon credits create a market for reducing greenhouse gas emissions by giving a monetary value to the cost of polluting the air. Emissions become an internal cost of doing business and are visible on the balance sheet alongside raw materials and other liabilities or assets.

Participating hotels obtain comprehensive reports on energy usage (including where energy is being wasted) and recommendations on operational and/or technological changes needed to maximize efficiency. CHENACT audits also complement or enhance certification processes for hotels that wish to participate in verified third party schemes. There are approximately 27 of such schemes that are listed on the Global Sustainable Tourism Council website.[2]

Energy-Saving Measures for Hotels

Energy costs (more specifically electricity rates) in the Caribbean are among the highest in the world, due to its dependence on oil-fired generation. These rates have been known to exceed US$0.40 per kilowatt-hour (kWh) in the Eastern Caribbean and up to US$0.51 in the northern islands. Figure 4.2 gives a breakdown of how hotels consume energy.

It should be noted that energy for laundry is relatively low. This is because large resorts generally outsource their laundry so it doesn't appear as a large energy cost for the property. In Barbados, for instance, annual energy costs were calculated as follows, based on the number of hotel rooms:

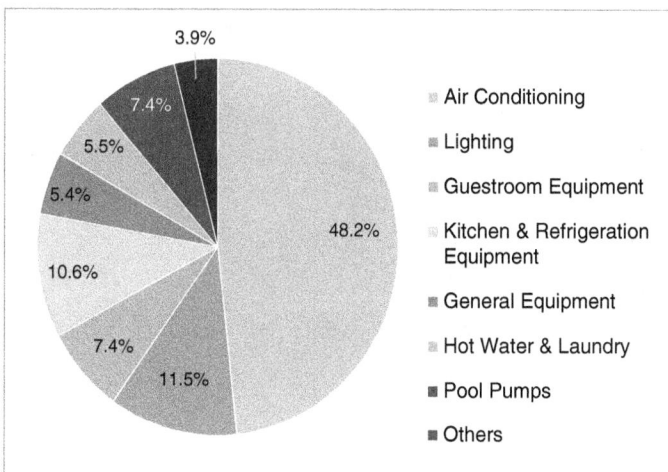

Figure 4.2 Breakdown of Energy Usage in Caribbean Hotels[3]

- Less than 50 rooms spend an average of US$113,500 on electricity;
- 51 to 100 rooms spend US$266,450;
- 101 to 200 rooms spend US$313,000; and
- More than 200 rooms spend an average of US$816,000.

From 2009 to 2012, CHENACT carried out energy audits of 47 hotels in Barbados, the Dominican Republic, Jamaica, and Trinidad and Tobago. These audits revealed that the potential for cost-effective energy savings in air conditioning, lighting, and other uses could be 30 to 50 percent of total electricity costs. Typically, hotels can recover their investments in energy efficiency in less than three years by installing the recommended energy-saving opportunities.[4]

To show the importance of renewable energy, CHENACT installed demonstration photovoltaic systems that are connected to the island's electricity grid in three hotels in Barbados. One of the hotels, the All Seasons Resort Europa, reported to CHENACT that it has calculated savings of approximately 10 percent on their bill with the installation of a 7.5-kW photovoltaic (PV) system.

Image 4.4.1 Example of Photo-Voltaic (PV) Systems installed on a hotel in Barbados.[5]

CHENACT has identified the following as the most practical and feasible technology options suitable for most of the hotels in the Caribbean:

- Air conditioning retrofit—inverter type variable refrigerant volume mini-splits;
- Guestroom energy controls—occupancy sensors, programmable thermostats;
- Public area lighting controls—occupancy sensors;
- Individual incandescent lamp replacement—compact fluorescent lamps (CFL) and light emitting diode (LED) lamps;
- Fluorescent tube lamps—T8 tube lamps with electronic ballasts and LEDs;
- Solar hot water (SHW) heating systems;
- Small renewable energy systems such as photovoltaic systems and wind systems;
- Energy-efficient freezers, refrigerators, cool rooms;
- Guest room energy-efficient mini-fridges, televisions;
- Office and guestroom energy-efficient equipment—televisions, computer monitors;
- Timers on pumps and motors;
- Photo-sensors and timers for outdoor lighting;
- Phase out of ozone depleting substances (refrigerant and air conditioning gases which impact the ozone layer) in hotels; and
- Energy Management Systems (EMS), which will enable hotels to put checks and balances to ensure the optimum use of energy.[ii]

What Do Energy Efficiency and Renewables in Caribbean Hotels Have to Do with Climate Change?

Given the predominance of oil-fired generation and high consumption levels of electricity, hotels are major contributors to greenhouse gas (GHG) emissions in the Caribbean, estimated at more than 3 million tons of carbon dioxide and other GHGs emitted per year.[iii]

[ii] CHENACT is developing this and will eventually put on their website.

[iii] Carbon dioxide equivalent (CO2e) is a measure used to compare the emissions from various greenhouse gases based upon their global warming potential. More information at http://climatechangeconnection.org/emissions/co2-equivalents/.

Energy efficiency and renewable energy have key roles to play in tackling climate change. Investments of US$433 million in cost-effective improvements in energy efficiency in Caribbean hotels could result in annual savings of US$271 million (or US$1.9 billion over seven years) in electricity costs and a reduction in emissions of 835 million tons of GHGs per year.[6]

Energy efficiency is one of the most important tools for avoiding climate change by reducing the use of fossil fuels. However, energy efficiency, renewable energy, and related demand management measures can also address some of the energy sector's vulnerabilities to climate change impacts:

- Deploying energy-efficient technologies in power generation, transmission, and distribution can help counteract the increased demand on and decreased output of power plants due to higher temperatures.
- Demand response programs and efficiency programs aimed at peak loads can help counteract the increase in peak demand due to increased use of air conditioning, and address the uncertainties in generation and consumption due to extreme weather, thus helping avoid the need for additional power plants.
- Builders can *future proof* hotels against predicted changes in weather patterns by ensuring long-lived characteristics such as orientation, insulation, and windows are appropriate for expected climate conditions.
- Resorts can reduce ambient temperatures and make hotels more efficient with cool or green roofs and the use of local building materials.
- Constructing distributed generation, especially efficient combined heat and power (CHP) plants, can provide secure electricity for large energy consumers or microgrids that are less subject to grid outages due to extreme weather.[iv]
- Water efficiency programs can address climate impacts on water resources and reduce energy use for pumping and treating water.

[iv] Distributed generation refers to power generation at the point of consumption. Combined Heat and Power (CHP) is a highly efficient process that captures and utilizes the heat that is a by-product of the electricity generation process.

If all the hotels in the Caribbean were to become energy efficient, a potential 884,000 tons of GHG emissions could be avoided annually.[7] Under the Plan of Action of CHENACT, the Caribbean tourism sector could potentially sell the carbon emission reductions and obtain funding for energy efficiency and renewable energy investments in the hotels in the region.[8]

Notes

1. The international agencies were the InterAmerican Development Bank (IDB), European Union (EU), United Nations Development Program (UNDP), and the German Agency for International Cooperation (GIZ). CHENACT. *Creating Sustainable Tourism for the Caribbean*. http://www.chenact.com/.
2. Global Sustainable Tourism Council. (2016). https://www.gst council.org/en/.
3. Figure Source: CHENACT.
4. CHENACT Final Report. (2012). http://www.chenact.com.
5. Image Source: CHENACT. (2014).
6. CHENACT Final Report. (2012).
7. CHENACT Final Report. (2012).
8. Two sources of funding for the Caribbean hotel sector are the Nationally Appropriate Mitigation Actions (NAMA) and Intentional Nationally Determined Contributions (INDC) programs. NAMA refer to any action that reduces emissions in developing countries and is prepared under the umbrella of a national governmental initiative. INDC are the reductions in greenhouse gas emissions that all countries published in the lead up to the Conference of Parties (CoP) in Paris. (2015). http://unfccc.int/focus/mitigation/items/7172.php. http://www4.unfccc.int/submissions/indc/Submission%20Pages /submissions.aspx.

Conclusions and Volume 2 Preview

Martha Honey

The Caribbean is the world's most tourism-dependent region, and in 2015, tourism in the Caribbean grew at a faster pace than any other region in the world. Most of the Caribbean's tourism infrastructure, many of its recreational activities, and three-quarters of its population are located along the coastlines. Although the Caribbean contributes less than 1 percent to global carbon emissions, the region's low-lying island states are already in the cross-hairs of a range of climate-related phenomena. These include environmental, social, and health problems such as increasingly fierce and frequent storms; ocean warming and sea-level rise; loss of critical habitat including corals, mangroves, and sea grasses; invasions of Sargassum seaweed; shortages of freshwater; and health outbreaks such as the Chikungunya and Zika viruses.

This book has focused on coastal hotels and resorts, shorelines, and beaches that are both the Caribbean's most important tourism assets and the frontline in battle to confront climate change. Through its range of essays and case studies, we have sought to answer a central question: *How coastal tourism must be planned, built, and operated in this era of climate change.* Two central truths have run through this volume. One is that many of these environmental, social, and health problems predate but are exacerbated by climate change. For decades, beaches and shorelines have been facing pressures from natural forces and human impacts, including destructive and shortsighted tourism development. Now climate change is accelerating these pressures. Oftentimes, we find that effective solutions to problems such as coral die-offs or freshwater shortages involve addressing multiple issues, not simply climate change.

The second truth is that many techniques for mitigating and adapting to climate change are part of the toolkit of sustainable tourism that has been honed over recent decades. Therefore, companies and coastal destinations adhering to the socially and environmentally responsible practices such as beach setbacks, soft engineering, renewable energy, water recycling and reduction, *green* architecture, and eco-certification programs are likely to be more resilient in coping with climate change.

But much more needs to be done to deepen and widen coastal tourism's responses to climate change. Climate change models predict that with a 2°C rise in global temperatures, 150 Caribbean coastal resorts will be lost and damages will total $22 billion a year by 2050. Despite these realities of coastal vulnerability and loss, author Judi Clarke writes that "complacency continues to be the norm in much of the Caribbean." As several of the case studies highlight, too many governments, resort developers and operators, sun and sand vacationers and vacation home owners, and beach and shoreline engineers have failed to fully grasp the projected impacts of climate change.

Tourism master planning and building today requires *a new normal* that incorporates present risks and climate change protections using smart planning, sustainable design, and responsible construction. Coastal tourism projects that incorporate sustainable and climate-change-resilient innovations have the ability to *bounce forward* with improvements and recovery after storms and flooding that also increase a property's value and life span.

This volume, which has focused on coastal hotels, beaches, and shorelines, is closely linked to a second volume centered on three auxiliary sectors—golf, local agriculture and cuisine, and airlines and airports—that are important components of the coastal tourism industry in the Caribbean. This second volume ends with an essay by Roger-Mark De Souza, "Challenges and Opportunities for the Caribbean," which serves as a comprehensive conclusion for both these coastal tourism volumes. De Souza summarizes the central themes from the two volumes and offers a roadmap for sustainable coastal tourism and successful adaptation and mitigation to climate change in the Caribbean.

Contributing Authors

Esteban Biondi

Esteban L. Biondi is associate principal at Applied Technology & Management (ATM) in West Palm Beach, Florida, where he provides specialized engineering, environmental, and consulting services for coastal resort projects and marinas. He has engineering degrees from Argentina and the United States and has directed over 100 consulting assignments in 30 countries.

Judi Clarke

Judi Clarke is a climate change adaptation specialist based in Barbados and held the post of Caribbean Regional Director of CARIBSAVE from July 2010 to July 2016. Judi has a special interest in community-based adaptation in vulnerable coastal communities in the Caribbean. She holds an MS in natural resources and environmental management and a BS in economics from the University of the West Indies.

Scott Curtis

Scott Curtis, professor in the Department of Geography, Planning, and Environment at East Carolina University (ECU), in Greenville, North Carolina, is affiliated with ECU's Center for Natural Hazards Research and Center for Sustainability. Curtis has published extensively on Caribbean climates and farmer vulnerabilities; and on the relationship between weather and coastal North Carolina tourism.

Loreto Duffy-Mayers

Loreto Duffy-Mayers is currently the regional program manager for the Caribbean Hotel Energy Efficiency and Renewable Energy Action (CHENACT) program based in Barbados and held the environmental manager position in several green hotels. She was educated at University College Dublin and the UK Institute of Marketing and has lived in Barbados since 1985.

Paul Guggenheim

Paul Guggenheim is the country representative for the Dominican Republic for the Social Sector Accelerator, a subsidiary of Counterpart International. Paul leads the implementation of a Coastal Community Resilience Framework building the capacity of coastal communities to confront the risks of climate change while generating alternative livelihoods.

Huili Hao

Huili Hao, PhD, serves as the research director of the Center for Sustainability, East Carolina University, in Greenville, North Carolina. Her research interests include sustainable community development and planning, sustainability, place attachment, hazards, vulnerability, and risk perceptions. Dr. Hao is also interested in applying spatial techniques to her research projects.

Denaye Hinds

Denaye Hinds leads OBMI's sustainability initiatives with extensive experience in sustainable infrastructure, tourism operations, training, and regulations for international standards and systems. She is based in Barbados and serves as technical director of CAST (Caribbean Alliance for Sustainable Tourism) and is a Climate Reality Leadership Corps trainer and LEED Accredited Professional.

Samantha Hogenson

Samantha Hogenson is the managing director of the Center for Responsible Travel. She was one of the first undergraduate students of geotourism and holds a master of tourism administration from The George Washington University, with an emphasis in sustainable tourism management. Samantha resides in Charleston, South Carolina.

Martha Honey

Martha Honey, PhD, is the executive director and co-founder of the Center for Responsible Travel (CREST). Over the last two decades, Martha has published and lectured widely on ecotourism, Travelers' Philanthropy, cruise and resort tourism, coastal and marine tourism, climate change, and certification issues. She holds a PhD in African history from the University of Dar es Salaam, Tanzania and an MA in African American history from Syracuse University. She worked as an international journalist for 20 years, based in East Africa and Central America.

Amy Kerr

Amy Kerr is the director of public relations for MP&A Digital & Advertising and has extensive experience in marketing and operations at top hospitality companies. Amy holds a bachelor's in communication from Randolph-Macon Woman's College and holds the Certified Hospitality Supervisor designation from the American Hotel & Lodging Association.

Jake Kheel

Jake Kheel is the vice-president of the Grupo Puntacana Foundation and oversees all social and environmental programs for Grupo Puntacana. Jake is also co-Director and Producer of *Death by a Thousand Cuts*, an award-winning documentary about deforestation on the island of Hispaniola. Jake has an MS in environmental management from Cornell University and BA from Wesleyan University.

Tisa LaSorte

Tisa LaSorte is the director of sales, marketing & administration and is on the executive management committee of Bucuti & Tara Beach Resort, in Aruba. Tisa's executive role includes collaborating in the implementation and communication of the resort's sustainability initiatives. She holds a bachelor's in communications management from Ithaca College.

Patrick Long

Patrick Long, PhD, is the founding director of the Centers for Sustainable Tourism at both the University of Colorado and East Carolina University. His research focuses on tourism planning, sustainable practices, rural tourism development, host community adjustments to tourism, and the impact of climate change on a tourism economy.

Andrea Pinabell

Andrea Pinabell was the vice-president of Sustainability for Starwood Hotels & Resorts until December 2016, where she was responsible for the company's sustainability strategy, integration, operation, and leadership across Starwood's 10 brands. Beginning in January 20917, Andrea became President of Southface, an Atlanta-based NGO which promotes market-based sustainable solutions in homes, workplaces, and communities. Andrea, a LEED AP, brought a global perspective and over 20 years of engineering, sustainability, philanthropy, and environmental management experience.

Michelle Rutty

Michelle Rutty, PhD, is an assistant professor of Sustainable Tourism at Michigan State University. Her research bridges social and natural scientific approaches to understand the implications of climate change for tourism. Her work has received international recognition, including awards from the Travel and Tourism Research Association and World Tourism Forum.

Index

OTHER TITLES IN TOURISM AND HOSPITALITY MANAGEMENT COLLECTION

Betsy Bender Stringam, *Editor*

- *The Good Company: Sustainability in Hospitality, Tourism and Wine* by Robert Girling

FORTHCOMING TITLES

- *Coastal Tourism, Sustainability, and Climate Change in the Caribbean, Volume II: Supporting Activities* Edited by Martha Honey with Samantha Hogenson
- *Marine Tourism, Climate Change, and Resiliency in the Caribbean, Volume I: Ocean Health, Fisheries, and Marine Protected Areas* by Kreg Ettenger with Samantha Hogenson
- *Catering and Convention Service Survival Guide in Hotels and Casinos* by Lisa Lynn Backus and Patti J. Shock

Announcing the Business Expert Press Digital Library

Concise e-books business students need for classroom and research

This book can also be purchased in an e-book collection by your library as

- a one-time purchase,
- that is owned forever,
- allows for simultaneous readers,
- has no restrictions on printing, and
- can be downloaded as PDFs from within the library community.

Our digital library collections are a great solution to beat the rising cost of textbooks. E-books can be loaded into their course management systems or onto students' e-book readers. The **Business Expert Press** digital libraries are very affordable, with no obligation to buy in future years. For more information, please visit **www.businessexpertpress.com/librarians**. To set up a trial in the United States, please email **sales@businessexpertpress.com**.

www.ingramcontent.com/pod-product-compliance
Lightning Source LLC
Chambersburg PA
CBHW050116210326
41519CB00015BA/3987